The Tragedy of Abundance

The Tragedy of Abundance

JEROME O. STEFFEN

UNIVERSITY PRESS OF COLORADO

Copyright © 1993 by the University Press of Colorado
P.O. Box 849
Niwot, Colorado 80544

10 9 8 7 6 5 4 3 2 1

The University Press of Colorado is a cooperative publishing enter-
prise supported, in part, by Adams State College, Colorado State
University, Fort Lewis College, Mesa State College, Metropolitan
State College of Denver, University of Colorado, University of
Northern Colorado, University of Southern Colorado, and Western
State College.

Library of Congress Cataloging-in-Publication Data

Steffen, Jerome O., 1942–
    The tragedy of abundance: myth restoration in American cul-
ture / Jerome O. Steffen.
        p.   cm.
    Includes bibliographical references and index.
    ISBN 0-87081-272-6 (alk. paper)
    1. Political culture — United States.   2. Wealth — United
States.   3. Messianism, Political — United States.   4. Idealism,
American.   5. Technology — Social aspects — United States.
I. Title.
JA84.U5S73 1992
306.2'0973 — dc20   92-36288
                                                        CIP

The paper used in this publication meets the minimum require-
ments of the American National Standard for Information
Sciences—Permanence of Paper for Printed Library Materials.
ANSI Z39.48–1984

∞

For Jo Ann
The joy of my life

Contents ❧

Preface ✦

I began thinking about the significance of abundance in the development of American culture when in 1980 I was invited to address a small conference of NASA scientists and other space-colonization enthusiasts. I was asked to speak on space as the next great frontier. Most of the participants assumed that I would share in their enthusiasm about space colonization and its potential for solving many current world problems. While doing research for my speech, however, I was struck by the unusually naive expectations that these scientists had for future space development. From my perspective as a historian, the pattern that unfolded as I read further on the subject seemed all too familiar. I had encountered it before, first in the writings of those expecting great things from the discovery and settlement of the New World in the sixteenth century, of those who made exaggerated claims for industrial technology in the mid-nineteenth century, and finally of those in the early twentieth century who had utopian expectations of scientific management and centralized authority.

My encounter with the literature on space colonization also led me to investigate futuristic accounts on additional subjects, such as genetic engineering, robotics, and high-tech communications. In all of the disciplines I encountered, the pattern of thinking was the same. The writing reflected the same tone of innocence and naivete that is so commonplace in American history.

It is quite apparent that Americans have developed a marked propensity for escaping unpleasant realities in their present lives through idyllic projections into the future. Furthermore, the process seems to be cyclical in nature. Two questions arise from this revelation. First, what has caused this innocence to develop and to persist for such a long time in American culture? Second, is there an encompassing process that can explain the evolution of American culture? This book is an attempt to answer these questions. Although I present my ideas in a direct manner, they are meant only to be suggestions for further debate. This study is not meant to be dogmatic but rather to bring relevant generalizations before the scholarly community.

I wish to thank the University of Oklahoma Research Council for a grant that has greatly facilitated my efforts to complete this project. I also wish to express my deepest gratitude to the grants and contracts office at the University of Oklahoma and its director, Brad Quinn, for introducing me to the world of word processing and for making equipment available to me. I am indebted to my wife, Jo Ann Steffen, who amidst a busy schedule of her own, found time to offer valuable editorial advice and most importantly for offering comfort and peace of mind to proceed with a project as difficult as this one. Finally, I owe a tremendous debt of gratitude to the large number of historians, sociologists, social psychologists, and political theorists from whose books and articles I have scavenged much data and many of my ideas.

JEROME O. STEFFEN

The Tragedy of Abundance

1.
The Pattern of Myth Restoration

Myths are common and important elements in all cultures. Ultimately, they are responsible for societal unity and cohesiveness. They explain the origins, the present, and the future of those who are immersed in their logic. They provide definitions of success and failure in the material world as well as in the spiritual realm of existence. They provide a link with supernatural forces, and with it an articulation of high ideals and lofty goals to which members can aspire. Finally, myths provide historical definition by providing explanations for national uniqueness and implicitly for national greatness.[1]

American myths are especially interesting because they were born out of, and continue to be nourished by, actual or perceived abundance. The five hundred years that followed the discovery of the New World in the fifteenth century witnessed in the United States the evolution of a most unusual society with most unusual ideas about people — what they are capable of and how they are supposed to be arranged socially, economically, and politically.

This study will concentrate on three myths that have been, and still are, especially important in American culture. First, the following chapters will show that Americans generally believe that most people are capable of dealing with freedom in a responsible manner. It is assumed, in other words, that the general interest of the nation is best served when a free citizenry encourages the pursuit of individual destinies without political or legal obstruction. Americans, regardless of how limited their knowledge on given issues, have demonstrated a great deal of confidence in their ability to determine not only what is best for themselves but also for their neighbors and even for the nation-state. The confidence that Americans have in themselves also translates into a belief that personal and national prosperity is a direct result of the freedom that Americans have to pursue their own destinies. Americans are not willing to entertain the notion that the nation's prosperity, to a large degree, is linked to the windfall created by the accidental discovery of continents in the fifteenth century that before were not known to exist.

Second, this study will illustrate that most Americans assume that material resources in America are infinitely available to those who work to acquire them if the system is allowed to function properly. Contrary to the pattern of economic distribution established over thousands of years of history, this ethos of growth and expansion persists in the belief that one element in society does not have to receive less in order for another element to receive more. Rapid change, so characteristic of American history, has fostered this notion because it has created an illusion that imperfection is only a temporary state for the wholesome, worthy citizen and that better conditions will exist in the future. This deep-seated notion, when combined with the myth of the rational free agent, has allowed Americans to believe that there is enough for all to have as much as their energies and abilities can acquire. Consequently, the average American is likely to assume that failure is the result of a lack of individual initiative or, on a larger scale, the fault of certain greedy elements in society that will not allow the system to function as it is supposed to.[2]

Third, scholars need not be reminded of the pervasive influence of manifest destiny and mission in American history. It is exaggerated well beyond the normal levels of ethnocentricity that is characteristic of all cultures. Since its inception, America has assumed that its way of life — manner of religious worship, form of government, economic system, and social order — is the only one that has any real claim to legitimacy. To be sure, gestures are made toward recognizing the merits of other cultures, but they are often patronizing at best, because in the final analysis these unfortunates are thought to be struggling with varying degrees of success to emulate the American way of life. In other words, it is assumed that the rest of the world is being remade in the image of America.[3]

It can safely be said that these myths were born of abundance and are an integral part of America's idealism and its persistent faith in the future. Certainly this is understandable given the nation's history of spectacular expansion and growth throughout the nineteenth century. Between 1790 and 1860 the population of the United States grew from four million to thirty-one million. Historically, dramatic population growth has resulted in diminished opportunity, want, and even starvation. The eminent economic historian Stuart Bruchey wrote that "had these millions been compelled to occupy the same space in which far smaller numbers had lived, insufferable densities might have resulted, with consequences for disease and mortality comparable to those of nineteenth-century Asia."[4]

Such was not the case in the United States because dramatic growth in population was matched by an even more dramatic growth in its resources. At the beginning of the nineteenth century, the public domain in the United States consisted of approximately 233 million acres. During the first half of the century, the nation added an additional 1,189,717 billion acres with the acquisition of Louisiana (1803), Florida (1819), Oregon (1846), Texas (1850), the Mexican Cession (1848), and, finally, the Gadsden Purchase (1853). On the eve of the Civil War, most of the resources between the first tier of states west of the Mississippi River and the Pacific Coast settlements had not yet been exploited; at that time, this region contained only 1 percent of the population.[5]

Between 1870 and 1910, the nation experienced its most dramatic population growth in a short period of time. The wave of European immigrants, coupled with a continuing rise in the birth rate, caused the nation's population to increase from 40 million to 92 million. Despite the dramatic increase in population, the United States continued to reflect its heritage of abundance. Real income nearly tripled during this period as a result of the development of western resources, most notably farming, ranching, and mining, plus, most significant of all, important development in the industrial sector of the economy.[6]

On the eve of World War I, the United States was the leading industrial nation in the world. Traditional as well as new industries experienced incredible growth when measured by almost any standard. Pig iron production increased from 1.8 million tons in 1870 to 10.3 million tons in 1890, while for the same period the output from steel manufacturing, a relatively new industry, increased from a mere 68,700 tons in 1870 to 4.2 million tons in 1910. The textile industry increased its consumption of cotton bales from 797 bales of cotton in 1870 to 2.6 million bales in 1891. The worth of materials used in the construction industry increased from $325 million in 1869 to over $1 billion in 1890.[7]

The manufacturers of a variety of consumer goods could boast of similarly impressive figures. The clothing industry increased its production from $230 million in 1869 to $589 million in 1890. The manufacturers of electrical appliances and equipment, a nearly nonexistent sector of the economy in 1870, produced goods worth $1.9 million in 1879 and $21.8 million in 1890. This dynamic economic pattern continued up to the 1930s when it was halted by the Great Depression. America's economic woes were eased, however, because of the ravenous demand for goods created by the outbreak of World War II. It must be kept in mind that the overall pattern of economic growth is the main concern here, not the short-term effects of recession and depression.[8]

I am not suggesting that all shared equally in the overall prosperity of the nation. It is a simple matter of fact that the distribution of resources in the United States has not changed dramatically since the beginning of colonization. In the years that immediately preceded the American Revolution, 40 percent of the wealth in the middle colonies of New York, New Jersey, and Pennsylvania was controlled by a mere 10 percent of the population. America's independence did little to change these conditions. In Chester County, Pennsylvania, for example, the wealthiest 10 percent of the population in 1794 controlled 40 percent of the region's resources, while the bottom 60 percent of the population in terms of material worth shared only 17.3 percent of the wealth. On the eve of the Civil War, little had changed. By 1860, despite the boom conditions created by the market revolution in the North, 70 percent of the nation's resources were still controlled by only 10 percent of the people.[9]

Industrialization had an even more devastating impact on the distribution of resources in the land of opportunity. In the first decade of the twentieth century, 60 percent of the nation's wealth was controlled by just 2 percent of the population; the bottom 65 percent of the population had to be content with only 5 percent of the wealth. Most Americans were ignorant of the fact that in 1910 seventy of the wealthiest Americans controlled one-sixteenth of the nation's wealth. Since World War II the top 20 percent of the population in terms of wealth has controlled no less than 40 percent of the nation's before-tax income, while the bottom 20 percent has controlled no more than 5.6 percent. The overall impact of abundance, however, was sufficient to create the perception of opportunity and with it an image of growth and progress in which all worthy and fit people could share equally.[10]

Although the myths born of abundance help explain American optimism, it must also be said that they are responsible for producing a persistent national neurosis because they portray a kind of existence that is so ideal that it must forever remain elusive. Alexis de Tocqueville noted this when he wrote in *Democracy in America* (1836) that although Americans live among the "happiest circumstances that the world affords," it appears "as if a cloud habitually hung upon their brow." Tocqueville thought Americans were unusually "serious" and "almost sad, even in their pleasures." The reason for such behavior, according to Tocqueville, is that Americans are "forever brooding over advantages they do not possess. It is strange to see with what feverish ardor the Americans pursue their own welfare, and to watch the vague dread that constantly torments them lest they should not have chosen the shortest path which may lead to it."[11]

The Epilogue of this book reveals the present tragedy and future danger that exist because of the nation's unwillingness to recognize that the ideology of free agency and opportunity is no longer applicable to a nation of more limited resources. No longer is overall economic growth and prosperity able to disguise inequity in American society. In the future, fundamental changes will be required in America's political, social, and economic outlook if class warfare and ideological strife, long associated with inequitable resource distribution, are to be avoided.

Various scholars have recognized the important relationship between growth and expansion and the evolution of American ideas and institutions. One of the earliest and most notable was Frederick Jackson Turner, who in his landmark essay, "The Significance of the Frontier in American History" (1893), described, albeit vaguely, a process that he believed was the major contributor to American character. He theorized that the presence of free land attracted individuals of varying backgrounds and nationalities to the frontier. The isolation of the frontier prompted the erosion of tradition and stimulated the development of new practices and ideas. Turner credited the frontier with producing a restless and staunchly individualistic people and, most important, a people deeply instilled with democratic principles.[12]

Walter Prescott Webb, in *The Great Frontier* (1964), incorporated abundance in an even broader interpretation of the evolution of American ideas and institutions. He noted that the discovery and settlement of the New World and the consequent reduction of the person-to-land ratio from 26.7 people per square mile to just 4.8 people per square mile threw the European political, social, and economic institutions that had been brought to the New World into a state of disarray. American development can thus be explained in terms of a "four hundred year boom" period, lasting from 1500 to 1900, during which the nation witnessed the rise of democratic institutions and their concomitant characteristics. Put simply, the perception of a limitless supply of resources made strong central authority appear excessive and therefore unnecessary. Conversely, Webb argues that by the beginning of the twentieth century the boom had ended as was reflected in the person-to-land ratio that had once again returned to 26.7 people per square mile. This resulted in central authority once again reasserting itself at the expense of individual freedom.[13]

Beginning in the mid-1950s, a number of other scholars in a variety of disciplines joined Webb in examining broadly defined themes in American history. Most notably, David Potter, in *People of Plenty* (1954), analyzed the wide-ranging effect of abundance on American political behavior, foreign policy, advertising practices, and even child-rearing customs.[14] Although much insight can be gained from Turner, Webb, and Potter, they stop short of addressing the actual process involved in maintaining and restoring endangered cultural myths. This is an important omission given that American myths, because of their naivete, have been difficult to sustain even in periods of relative peace and prosperity. Thus it can be argued that myth restoration has been and still is an important part of American history. Insights into the myth-restoration process itself can be gained from anthropologists, who have long viewed revivalism and cargo cults, as well as millenarian and messianic movements, in this context. American historians, however, have not been as interested in the subject.[15]

The chapters that follow will argue that myth restoration is one of the most distinctive characteristics in American cultural development and that the phenomenon is cyclical in nature. Each cycle begins with eager anticipation of some future development that is expected to usher in a new golden age. The scenario of the future typically depicts a fair and more equitable society in which the gap between the rich and poor is greatly diminished. It is anticipated that there will be greater opportunities for all citizens to achieve higher levels of material comfort and that citizens will have more leisure time, which will be used to realize greater spiritual, aesthetic, and intellectual enlightenment.

Unfortunately, these naive expectations are inevitably dashed by reality, thus leading to periods of widespread disillusionment that first appear on the fringes of the culture before eventually consuming the attention of the majority of citizens. I will demonstrate that in American history there were three periods of unusually high expectation followed by three periods of widespread disillusionment, which led to dramatic increases in the number of people who knowingly or unwittingly engaged in a wide range of experiments designed to achieve the kind of life described in myth.

The chapters that follow will analyze experiments in education, pseudoscience, health, diet, and exercise regimens, as well as in cleansing movements associated with perceived alcohol and drug abuse and rampant immorality. Removing unwanted people, an extreme form of nativism, will also be treated in this book as a cleansing movement designed to help align the nation with its self-image. The aforementioned themes have been chosen because they have not been studied as therapeutic aids to myth restoration. Pseudoscience and changes in education, health, diet, and exercise have traditionally been viewed in terms of reform. This study, however, emphasizes their role in assuring their followers that the American dream is still viable and worth pursuing and that it can be achieved with the proper therapeutic application.

Ironically, within a decade or so of the beginning of each of the three periods of experimentation and reform, one witnesses a backlash against many of the same experiments that were originally looked to with such great anticipation. At this juncture, the process begins all over again as Americans, slowly but inexorably, become enamored of some new development that they expect will usher in yet another future golden age.

Chapters 2 through 4 deal with three consecutive cycles of myth restoration. Chapter 2 focuses on the disillusionment and experimentation that developed as a result of the unfulfilled expectations associated with newly discovered places. This cycle began with the wild speculations that followed the discovery of the New World. Imaginations were inflamed as never before when Europeans gained knowledge of a vast tract of land that was previously unknown. Americans continued this pattern each time a new frontier was opened for settlement. The pages of American history are littered with the exaggerated claims and false hopes of people who looked with great anticipation to the Ohio Valley, to the Upper Mississippi Valley, to the Gulf Plains, to the far Northwest, and finally even to the semiarid Great Plains.

Chapter 3 focuses on the disillusionment and experimentation that followed the failed expectations of the age of industrial technology. Ironically, Americans welcomed industrialization even though their image of similar developments in Europe was quite negative. Americans saw industrialized Europe as a place where crowded cities were thought to fester with filth and degradation and where women and children were being exploited by callous, greedy, and uncaring industrialists. Americans, on the other hand, believed that industrialization in their nation would consist of small factories quietly nestled in peaceful little villages surrounded by farms and rolling countryside. It was widely believed that, much like the western frontiers of an earlier time, the machine would usher in an age of greater opportunity and equality, an age that would provide more leisure time for the average citizen to pursue aesthetic and spiritual enlightenment.

As the twentieth century dawned, Americans were well aware of the fact that their nation was not developing in a manner consistent with their nation's exalted self-image. Americans did not, however, have to abandon the sacred myths of free agency and unlimited opportunity, because they were told by the intelligentsia that the failure of the American dream was the result of a few greedy industrialists who had managed to frustrate the natural order of a free people equally competing for the spoils of the land of opportunity.

Chapter 4 unveils yet another round of naive expectations, this time stimulated by the principles of scientific management. Now it was the management expert who was expected to bring the American dream to fruition. Americans were told that the nation's expectations of itself would at last be realized because it was felt by many that management experts, unlike the greedy industrialists, would be indifferent to special-interest groups. It was also anticipated that these experts would use scientific knowledge to make more efficient use of the nation's resources and that this would result in more freedom, greater material abundance, and a more enlightened citizenry. During the past three and a half decades, the Eden of the expert has been under constant attack. Today bureaucrats, the legacy of scientific management, have replaced industrialists as the scapegoats for the nation's inability to realize the idyllic society described in myth.

Chapter 5 points out that today there are already signs that some Americans may be ready to look to the future once again as an escape from present imperfection. The books and articles that have emerged from the pens of a small band of enthusiastic futurists over the past several decades make it clear that high-tech communication, robotics, genetic engineering, and space colonization are likely to be the focus of the next round of Edenic expectations. It is not surprising that the rhetoric of enthusiasts in these fields echoes the naive expectations of those in the past who looked to other future developments with the same degree of innocence.

Americans today, just as in the past, are living a tragic paradox. On the one hand, they work feverishly to bring about change because of the abundance-inspired belief that change equals progress. Yet, at the same time, most individuals are incapable of anticipating the consequences of change and are ill equipped to deal realistically with them. Abundance has provided numerous opportunities for America to look to the future with hope, yet, ironically, abundance as the catalyst for rapid change has threatened to expose its most sacred myths. As a result, Americans have been and still are caught in a cyclical pattern of myth restoration that they have not yet been forced to abandon. It can be argued that abundance has caused Americans to cling stubbornly to naive myths, which has slowed their maturation as a people. Historian David F. Noble noted with great insight that America is "a remarkably dynamic country that goes nowhere." It is a nation in which "everything changes, yet nothing moves. Every new seemingly bold departure ends by following an already familiar path." [16]

2.
The Western Paradise

EXPECTATIONS

The discovery of the New World at the end of the fifteenth century
was an event that caused human imagination to run wild. What
great mysteries did this strange new land harbor? What did its
discovery mean to the future of humankind? The sixteenth-cen-
tury Spanish quest for the many envisioned El Dorados in the
New World is an early example of the instinct to fantasize about
that which is little known. British encounters with the New World
in the early seventeenth century were not as flamboyant as the
Spanish quest for gold a century earlier, but the British were
equally naive in their expectations of the unknown.

   The British were most excited about the soil and the flora
and fauna. In 1584 the respected traveler Richard Hakluyt described the soil of the new-found paradise in North America as
being inexhaustible. In his opinion, it was possible to grow
anything in great quantities for as long as one chose to do so.[1]

   In addition, there were reports that some of the plants in
the New World had incredible medicinal value. Men of medicine
spoke of finally being able to cure diseases that had eluded their
profession since the beginning of time. John Frampton's book
Joyfull Newes Out of the Newe Founde World (1588) optimistically
told of the "rare and singular virtues" of the herbs, trees, and
plants of the New World. Frampton predicted that the flora of the
New World would "bringeth such present remedy for all diseases
as may seem altogether incredible."[2]

There was also a spiritual dimension to early expectations
of the New World. Primitive land and primitive people conjured
up images of lost paradise as Europeans were moved by the
possibility of finding an inner peace not realized since Adam and
Eve had been exiled from the Garden of Eden. Although human
longings for an Edenic existence are universal and timeless,
demonstrations of this instinct are more pronounced in some
periods than in others. The initial encounter with the New World
in the sixteenth and seventeenth centuries inaugurated one of
those periods of extreme excitement in human history.[3]

On a less sensational level, but no less important, the New
World also titillated the imaginations of the landless, who could
now dare to imagine themselves not only as small landowners
but possibly even as landed aristocrats. The distinction between
the two levels of land ownership is important because as a
member of the landed aristocracy the successful immigrant
could look forward to a prominent social standing and to being
viewed as a person of good breeding, refinement, temperance,
and sound judgment. Virginia, for example, was thought to be a
place where barns and granaries were overflowing with bountiful
harvests and where one could "live freely . . . without sergeants
or courtiers or lawyers or intelligencers. You may be an alderman
there and never be a scavenger, you may be a nobleman and
never be a slave."[4]

The American colonial experience ended with the War of
Independence in 1776, but the propensity for making idyllic
projections about unknown places did not. The tendency continued because of the perception of an almost limitless amount of
unexploited land west of the Appalachian Mountains. Initially it
was little-known places, such as Kentucky and Ohio, that much
like the New World earlier on assumed an exotic and mysterious
air filled with endless possibilities. One of the earliest accounts
of Kentucky appears in the *Jesuit Relations* (1663). The author,
Hierosme Lalemant, even though he had never been there,
reported that Kentucky was a place with "a climate that is always

temperate — a continual Spring and Autumn, as it were." The soil of the region was so fertile that the Indian corn there had a "stalk of such extraordinary thickness and height that one would take it for a tree." It was a place about which "one could almost say of it within bounds, what the Israelite discoverers said of the Promised Land." In the late eighteenth century, noted traveler Timothy Flint described Kentucky as a place that was truly "the home of all that is good, fertile, happy and great."[5]

Although most people did not actually migrate to the West, its mere existence was a major contributor to the optimism and high expectations many Americans had about the future and the new places in the West. The goal of most of those who migrated to the frontier was similar to that of those who came to the New World several centuries earlier — to acquire enough land to enter the sacred realm of the landed aristocracy. Citizens caught up in the vision of an abundant frontier expected their lives to be filled with leisure and refinement. They sought greater social promi- nence, more political power, and, of course, the luxury usually reserved only for elites. These yearnings were captured beauti- fully in James Paulding's poem "The Backwoodsman" (1818), which tells of the transformation of its main character, Basil, after he had migrated from New York to Ohio. In New York Basil was depicted as a "hardy swain" of the "lowly rural train," who "barely kept his family fed." However, after migrating to Ohio his circum- stances changed dramatically.[6]

> Old Basil — for his head is not grown gray
> Waxes in wealth and honours every day;
> Judges, general, congressman, and half a score of
> goodly offices, and titles more
> Reward his worth, while like a prince he lives.[7]

Although life did improve for the majority of those who migrated to the Old Northwest, a shortage of capital and labor would insure that only a few would actually reach the ranks of the landed aristocracy, and certainly almost all failed to find the illusive idyllic life portrayed in frontier mythology. The Edenic view of the West, however, did not die in the forests and meadows of the Old Northwest. A new opportunity to fantasize about little-known places was provided by Oregon and California beginning in the mid-1840s. One account portrayed Oregon as a place where there exists "everything that can cheer, sustain, and elevate the human condition; everything for improvement and enjoyment . . . and everything that can gladden the heart in better hopes beyond the grave." [8]

The claims made about Oregon, however, paled in comparison to those made about California. In addition to the wealth associated with the gold rush, this Pacific paradise was thought to offer unparalleled opportunities for health and happiness. "If a man were to ask of God a climate," wrote one enthusiast, "he would ask just such a one as that of California." One claim that popularly circulated in the East insisted that "there was but one man in California that ever had a chill there, and that was a matter of so much wonderment . . . that they went eighteen miles in the country to see him shake." Even more incredible was a story that told of a man who had lived for 250 years before moving to a new location, whereupon death overtook him. When he was returned to California for burial, life was restored to him and he was "reinvested with all the vigor and beauty of early manhood." [9]

It is not suggested here that the fanciful descriptions of life in California were actually believed. It is argued, however, that they reinforced deep-seated notions of a much more serious nature. Such tales, although silly in the telling, reinforced the belief and the hope that "tomorrow" and "out there" were dimensions in which the good life could be found. The inflated tales of the West are thus a part of the timeless and universal process by which humankind has sought to escape imperfection.

Unfortunately, these same beliefs were an integral part of the underlying rationalizations of manifest destiny. *Manifest destiny* was a term used in the early nineteenth century to justify aggressive westward expansion, which was a mixture of greed and racism. In the nineteenth century, this was directed mostly at Hispanics and Native Americans and the land that they occupied. According to Frederick Merk, a strong sense of mission was also a part of American expansionism because many Americans were consumed with the notion that their nation was providentially assigned to uplift and regenerate the world beginning with the inferior civilizations still in existence on the North American continent. Merk argued that the mission concept made aggressive expansion appear to be an unselfish act that could be endorsed enthusiastically. It also allowed farmers, ranchers, railroad companies, town developers, land speculators, the federal government, and others with vested interests to expand aggressively into western territories without contradicting the basic tenets of freedom and equality.[10]

In addition to dynamic geographic expansion and economic growth, the first half of the nineteenth century witnessed a phenomenon known as the rise of the common man. In general, the early nineteenth century saw the weakening of central authority and an increase in local autonomy. In the political arena, state after state adopted universal suffrage and with it an acceptance of the notion that voting was no longer the exclusive domain of property owners, just as leadership was no longer reserved only for the aristocrat. In similar fashion, the legal system was expected to promote individual freedom aggressively, especially freedom to make economic decisions unencumbered by regulation. The democratization of law was most clearly reflected in the dramatic increase in the number of judgeships that became elective positions and thus fell under the direct control of the people. [11]

DISILLUSIONMENT

The early nineteenth century was a time when numerous contradictions surfaced in American culture. During this period Americans had every right to believe that they were well on their way to creating the ideal society. There existed a general, albeit vague, perception that the economy was booming and that people had more freedom than ever before to pursue the abundant resources that surrounded them. Yet, at the same time, the early nineteenth century was a period of growing uneasiness among the citizenry of America in a variety of areas affecting their lives. There was, of course, the growth of political parties, something Americans had not yet become comfortable with because they symbolized division and factionalism. Also the nation feared for its continued existence in the face of the hostile European nations that surrounded it in the New World. Equally serious, the nation's future appeared threatened because of the growing sectional tensions between the North and the South.[12]

On a more abstract yet no less important level, the naive American myths meant that people were already in pursuit of an elusive and unachievable kind of life that was most often rooted in economic gain. Alexis de Tocqueville wrote that in America "men easily attain a certain equality of condition, but they can never attain as much as they desire. It perpetually retires before them, yet without hiding itself from their sight and retiring draws them on. At every moment they think they are about to grasp it; it escapes at every moment from their hold." Tocqueville concluded that "they are near enough to see its charms, but too far off to enjoy them; and before they have fully tasted its delights, they die."[13]

Ironically, some Americans were fearful of the very objective that they strove so hard to achieve — prosperity. In 1836 Samuel Osgood wrote that "the dangers which our nation fears, and the trouble it has experienced, have been occasioned in great measure by our national prosperity" because it threatened that which was thought to be one of the nation's most enduring strengths, "republican plainness." According to evangelist Lyman Beecher, "Without some self-preserving moral power" America's abundance would provide the "fuel for the fire which is destined to consume us. The greater our prosperity the shorter its duration, and the more tremendous our downfall unless the moral power of the gospel shall be exerted to arrest those curses which have destroyed other nations."[14]

Americans — East and West, rural and urban, young and old, upper and lower class — were faced with new, and often times bewildering, developments that had come upon them with such rapidity that they could not possibly understand their meaning. The West, a source of so much optimism and pride earlier, had become by the middle of the second decade of the nineteenth century a source of great anxiety not only for those who had migrated there but also for some easterners who viewed the events there from a distance. National political leaders were fearful that these frontier settlements, once removed from the influence of the federal government, could easily fall prey to foreign intrigue. Arthur St. Clair, the first governor of Northwest Territory, wrote that the citizens in his charge were "a multitude of indigent and ignorant people . . . ill qualified to form a constitution and a government for themselves." He warned that "at present they seem attached to the General Government, it is in fact but a passing sentiment, easily changed or even removed and certainly not strong enough to be counted upon."[15]

Theologians and educators were also upset by accounts, often exaggerated, that depicted frontier societies as strongholds of barbarism. America's sense of mission made frontier reform an urgent issue. If America was responsible for delivering the world from its morass of imperfection, then it would be the frontier that would serve as the cutting edge. If those on the frontier had succumbed to barbarity, then the mission was surely in jeopardy. Evangelist Lyman Beecher warned that if frontier reform did not take place, it would be impossible for the nation "to lead the way in the moral and political emancipation of the world." In addition, there were those who were fearful that the violence and debauchery of the West, as it was perceived to exist, would eventually filter back to the East and affect the behavior of those in this more settled region.[16]

Life for those actually residing in the West was not without its troubling aspects either. For many, it was a psychological burden to begin life anew without the security and comfort of friends, relatives, and familiar surroundings. In addition, the isolation of the frontier made it appear as if officials in Washington were indifferent to their needs. Frontier isolation reinforced a tendency toward paranoia because of persistent rumors of Indian attacks and foreign invasion.

In addition to the frontier concerns just discussed, the early stages of industrialization in the Northeast provided yet other sources of anxiety. Thousands flocked to the city expecting opportunity without realizing that the realities of urban industrial living would assault the pastoral pace and texture of life with which they were accustomed. Some experienced or witnessed labor exploitation along with instances of poverty and crime. Excessive alcohol consumption and prostitution were also sources of concern because they were more visible in urban settings. It is clear that Americans were intellectually unprepared to live comfortably with the consequences of democratization. Rather than a republic of virtuous citizens pursuing their own individual destinies in a free and open society, America, to many of its citizens, had become a place with unacceptable levels of immorality and economic injustice.

EXPERIMENTATION AND MYTH RESTORATION

The bewildering array of reforms that occurred during the 1830s is a measure of the breadth and depth of the disillusionment in America. Not all Americans, however, perceived the nation's problems from the same perspective. Thus their efforts to correct the problems of society also were scattered over a wide range of activities, including those featured in this discussion — education, pseudoscience, health regimens, and various expressions of nativism.

Although on the surface the various reforms of the early nineteenth century appear to be quite diverse, in fact they were quite similar in their assumptions and in the role they played in myth restoration. Americans, because of their individualistic mind-set, did not entertain systemic reforms or measures that would legislatively coerce citizens as a whole into behaving in a more acceptable manner. Americans believed that national rejuvenation was closely linked to individual rejuvenation and that this redemptive process was to be a strictly voluntary matter. It could be argued that the reforms that were undertaken in the early nineteenth century were acceptable to Americans because they helped Americans to continue to believe that an open and free society was possible and that people could use their freedoms responsibly.

Education was a key reform element in the early nineteenth century and therefore also was seen as a key element in the creation of the America envisioned in myth. Educational reformers addressed the same concerns addressed by other reformers of the period — personal debilitation, factionalism, and self-serving politics, as well as excessive competitiveness that was thought to be a major contributor to economic injustice. Horace Mann, whose name is synonymous with early nineteenth-century education, wrote that "with every generation, fortunes increase on the one hand, and some new privation is added to poverty on the other. We are verging towards those extremes of opulence and penury, each of which unhumanize the mind." Educational reformers were driven by the notion that an educated citizenry would behave less selfishly and that it would also be less susceptible to the selfish interests of others. Mann was obviously reflecting the American sense of mission when he wrote that universal education will "obliterate factious distinctions in society," thus allowing America to fulfill its mission as "a model and pattern for nations, a type of excellence to be admired and followed by the world."[17]

The failures to which Mann referred were never discussed in systemic terms, at least not in the mainstream of society. There was no need to look to the system if failure could be attributed to individual weakness. Schoolbooks commonly explained economic failure in terms of laziness and immorality. "Poverty is the fruit of idleness," counseled one early nineteenth-century reader, while another explained that "declining prosperity is the usual attendant of degenerate morals in individuals, in families, and in larger communities." Temperance themes took up more than their share of space in school texts. Referring to alcohol, one schoolbook warned the reader that "if you use that beverage beggary will be your destiny."[18]

If education served as an antidote to economic failure, so too was it viewed as protection against freedom digressing into an ugly contest between self-serving interest groups. Lyman Beecher warned "that our intelligence and virtue will falter and fall back into a dark minded, vicious populace — a poor, uneducated reckless mass of infuriated animalism." "We must educate!" he wrote. "We must educate! or we must perish by our own prosperity."[19]

Although there was a foreboding tone to that which was passed on through textbooks, there was an underlying optimism as well. The confidence of the age was reflected in the manner in which truth was pursued. Ultimate or higher forms of truth were gained through intuition and common sense, not through knowledge and reasoning. With the exception of providing the rudiments of the three R's, education existed to pass on truths already known to responsible citizens. Knowledge that had no practical purpose was considered to be a useless exercise. "While other nations are wasting the brilliant efforts of genius in monuments of ingenious folly, to perpetuate their pride," one text stated, "the Americans according to the true spirit of republicanism, are employed almost entirely in works of public and private utility." Impractical knowledge merely cluttered up the mind and prevented people from using their natural intuitive powers to pursue their own destinies.[20]

What of the threat posed to the elite elements in American society by the democratization of education? One text was confident that public education would stabilize the social order rather than upset it. "Nor is it at all more rational to suppose that a judicious education of the poor, conducted to any attainable extent, will be liable to abuse in their hands, and lead them to forget their station and their duty, than it will have similar effects on those who are nourished in the lap of affluence."[21]

Although Horace Mann warned about the gap between the rich and the poor, temporary poverty was a generally accepted condition. Some schoolbooks counseled that poverty was not without its virtues, or as one text put it, "Poverty is oftener a blessing than a curse." Students were reminded that the wealthy are often burdened with responsibility and find themselves suffering greater temptation, thus making it more difficult to achieve the rewards of heaven. Permanent poverty, however, was disconcerting and not viewed with sympathy because the condition was generally viewed to be the fault of the individual.[22]

In the end, the importance of education, according to historian Lawrence Cremin, rested upon its ability to provide "a sense of comity, community, and common aspiration to a people who were increasing in number, diversifying in origin, and insistently mobile." Cremin argued that education united "the symbols of Protestantism, the values of the Old and New Testaments, *Poor Richard's Almanack,* and the *Federalist* papers, and the aspirations asserted on the Great Seal." All of these elements are tightly woven into the three myths of concern to this discussion.[23]

Education was also manifested in institutions that fostered greater public awareness. The American Lyceum was just such an institution. The lyceum movement attracted Americans from across the nation to local churches, schoolhouses, and town halls to listen to lectures on topics that ranged from advice on how to get rich to the problem of rampant immorality and how to deal with it. The lyceum provided its share of misinformation, but this mattered little because speakers, whether they were aware of it or not, were dealing with matters that had become sources of great anxiety to those in attendance. The lyceum was also important because, like revival meetings, it was a forum for cathartic relief. Individuals, through their participation in discussions, could unburden themselves of personal fears and concerns. Historian Carl Bode reports of these lectures that their "organization, length, and style resembled that of the religious homily."[24]

Other Americans saw other reasons for America's shortcomings. If too many people were behaving immorally and unethically or were not able to compete effectively for the spoils of the New World, then, some reasoned, physiological shortcomings were at the root of such failures. Desperate for explanations, many turned to health evangelists and pseudoscientific therapists beginning in the 1830s to find plausible explanations for their personal plights and for the failure of the nation as a whole.

Sylvester Graham was the most popular of those preaching the gospel of health. Graham was particularly concerned about the dangerous implications of inferior bread. As a New Englander, he was concerned about the excessive amount of wheat that was being imported from the Ohio Valley. He considered this wheat to be inferior because it was grown in soil that was unnaturally fertilized with animal dung. Equally disturbing to him, too many women were abandoning their traditional roles as mothers and wives to work in newly emerging factories. Thus, in matters such as bread baking, their loving hands had been replaced with those of profit-oriented commercial bakers, who had little regard for the moral and physical state of those who purchased their bread.[25]

Like today's purveyors of healthy living, Graham charged that bread was too often laced with "chemical agents," such as "alum, sulphate of zinc, sub-carbonate of magnesia [and] sulphate of copper," to compensate for the inferior flour that was being used. Consequently, he urged his followers to use locally grown whole wheat, husk and all, to produce a "more substantial and health giving bread." From Graham's perspective, inferior bread was symbolic of many other problems in the nation. He, like the educational reformers, was unwittingly reacting to the threat that change had imposed upon his naive and innocent view of America. He, too, was reacting to a society that he felt had become riddled with inequality and immorality. His contribution to myth restoration came in the form of a comprehensive health regimen that he assumed would elevate the moral and ethical level of his fellow citizens and eventually the nation as a whole.[26]

Graham believed that there was a direct connection between the overstimulation of the body's organs and mental and physical stability. Specifically, he believed that eating and drinking the wrong things in excess aroused sexual desires, which in turn caused the body's organs to be overstimulated and stressed to the limit. Sexual stimulation, according to Graham, caused a torrent of blood to flow "into the brain, stomach, lungs and other important organs," leading to "emaciation, lassitude, general chilliness, coldness of the extremities, and great debility." In extreme cases, the heart might even burst "causing sudden death in the unclean act." Such frightful activity was the source of almost every human ailment, ranging from baldness and bad teeth to "asthma, pulmonary consumption and even tuberculosis."[27]

Exercise was also critical to Graham's regimen for curbing sexual appetites because it prevented blood from collecting in the genital regions of the body. Accordingly, he advised people "to go to the gymnasium," to "swing upon the wooden horses . . . to walk, run, and jump or labor on the farm." He also urged them to engage in horseback riding but not without a stern warning that if such activity should result in "involuntary emissions, this mode of activity must be avoided."[28]

Graham's solutions to America's problems were, in the broadest sense, the result of coming to grips with living in an open and free society. His idyllic view of America was challenged by the competitive struggles that were unfolding around him. A world of injustice and poverty belonged to other places and times and was supposed to have little to do with the democratic experiment that was unfolding in the New World. Graham lived during a period when the agricultural society of New England had to deal with changes associated with the early stages of industrialization. Urbanization, a more heterogeneous population, and the changing roles of women and children were but a few of the developments that Graham, like most Americans, was incapable of fully understanding. Consistent with key American myths concerning individualism, free agency, and abundance, Graham assumed that national redemption was first and foremost a matter of individuals coming to grips with their problems. He brought enlightenment to them, and they would voluntarily choose to correct their deficiencies. As the number of enlightened individuals multiplied, the America envisioned in myth would move closer to becoming a reality.

Phrenology, a diagnostic technique that served a therapeutic role, also enjoyed considerable popularity in the early nineteenth century. Like the Graham system, it had wide appeal because it was based on the belief that a confusing array of social problems stemmed from a single cause — physical and mental deterioration in the fast-paced, helter-skelter world of the early nineteenth century.

Phrenology assumed, as did the Graham system, that physiology was related directly to behavior. It was more precise, however, in defining the exact relationship between the two. The pseudoscience identified thirty-seven distinct and independent units in the brain that were believed to represent different human characteristics, both positive and negative. In addition, each area of the brain, with its corresponding characteristics, was linked to specific organs in the body. An underdevelopment or an overdevelopment of these organs was felt to affect the development of the corresponding portions of the brain and the behaviors associated with them. Thus, it was believed that mental instability was linked directly to the natural development of the body's organs. Therefore, it was important that these organs not be impeded artificially through the use of alcohol, caffeine, and tobacco or by wearing tight-fitting belts or corsets.[29]

When phrenology was originally introduced from Europe, it was strictly an abstract science. In the United States, however, it gained widespread popularity as a predictive science that offered the hope that people could once again control their own destinies. Phrenologists claimed to be able to predict character based on the protrusions on the human skull. These protrusions were indications of which portions of the brain were overdeveloped or underdeveloped. Given the eagerness of Americans to learn about the future there was no shortage of traveling flimflam artists ready and willing to separate people from their hard-earned money. In addition, over one hundred thousand copies of phrenology books, complete with easy-to-follow diagrams of the brain, were purchased.

Reputable phrenologists did exist, however, and some were considered to be among the most respected members of the community. Their skills were widely used by businessmen in their hiring practices. The mobility of Americans made it difficult for businessmen to hire people based on personal knowledge of them or their families. Consequently, phrenology was used to screen job applicants, in much the same way as the polygraph is used today. It was not uncommon to find help-wanted ads that required phrenological reports. The following ad ran in an 1847 edition of the *New York Sun:*

> An Apprentice Wanted — A stout boy not over 15 years of age, of German or Scotch parents, to learn a good but difficult trade. N.B. — it will be necessary to bring a recommendation to his abilities from Messrs. Fowlers and Wells, Phrenologists, Nassau Street. Apply corner of West and Franklin Streets.[30]

Horace Greeley tried to convince the railroads to use phrenological reports in their hiring practices. "Such men can be obtained," Greeley wrote, "perhaps not at the lowest market price, but at prices somewhat equivalent to their required capacities, and nominal in the value of life, limb and property considered. But how? By the aid of phrenology, and not otherwise."[31] Although Greeley's advice was not followed, the mere suggestion by a prominent newspaperman that phrenology be employed in an important industry is an indication that it was taken seriously.

It can be seen that the assumptions and the problem-solving techniques of the educational and physiological therapists of the early nineteenth century were the same. In each case, their reform efforts were directed at the individual; improvement would come about as the result of a voluntary effort. Most reformers did not see the subtle connection between their efforts. Religious leaders, for example, objected to phrenology because they perceived it to be a science that reduced humans to the level of machines. This was disturbing to theologians because it seemed to contradict their beliefs in free will. After all, if humans were at the mercy of their environment, then, implicitly, they were not responsible for their sins. Yet phrenologists were unwittingly engaged in a quest with goals very similar to those of the theologians. In fact, historian John Davies writes: "American phrenology became a sort of religion itself, a kind of optimistic and sentimental deism. It appropriated the logic and techniques of evangelical Protestantism — its lecturers received a 'call' to the 'faith,' designated themselves 'missionaries,' conducted 'revivals,' distributed 'tracts' and made 'converts.' "[32]

Nativistic expressions can also be seen as reform efforts directed at creating the kind of America envisioned in myth. In the strictest sense, of course, the instinct is harmless enough. The term applies to the perpetuation of an indigenous culture, as opposed to a foreign culture. In one of its most extreme forms, however, it must be viewed as a cleansing movement that in some instances led to direct and indirect persecution of certain groups of people who were considered to be incompatible with the nation's self-image. The credibility of groups espousing nativism seems to vary with the degree of anxiety and fear that exists in a society at any given time. The early nineteenth century was a time when it was possible for those who assaulted Catholics and Mormons, two of the most popular targets for persecution, to be taken seriously by more people than ever before.

Ironically, Mormons were responding to the same fears and anxieties as their detractors, and they, like their Christian brethren, looked to a higher authority for order and predictability in the world. The social structure of the Mormons, however, was too communal to be tolerated in an individualistic society. As a result of their social conventions and practices, such as polygamy, they suffered persecution wherever they attempted to establish their communities. Forced to flee from Ohio, Illinois, and Missouri, they eventually found a refuge in the region of the Great Salt Lake in Utah.[33]

For some caught up in the hysteria of nativism, a wave of Irish Catholic immigrants to the urban areas of the Northeast prompted renewed fears that foreign infestation was the cause of the nation's shortcomings. More specifically, the Irish were perceived to be a major cause of the lack of economic opportunity and the moral decline in the nation. In addition to the immediate economic and moral threat that the Irish posed, their church was looked upon with disdain because of its hierarchical structure and its elaborate set of rituals. These practices stood in odious contrast to the nondeferential, individualistic Christian doctrines that had come to dominate American thinking. One could learn about these hideous Catholics through sermons, pamphlets, and books with such intriguing titles as *Priest's Prison for Women, The Escaped Nun, Open Convents,* and *Nunneries and Popish Seminaries Dangerous to the Morals and Degrading to the Character of a Republican Community.*[34]

The sentiments of such tracts were reinforced by prominent community leaders such as Samuel Morse, who was especially concerned about papal imperial designs on America. Morse was moved to ask: "How is it possible, that the foreign turbulence imported by ship loads that riot, and ignorance in hundreds of thousands of human priest-controlled machines, should suddenly be thrown into our society and not produce here turbulence and excess? Can one throw mud into pure water and not disturb its clearness?"[35]

Reflecting the confusion of the time, some frightened citizens organized groups to counter the existence of yet other reform groups. For example, an increase in the membership rolls of the Masons, a secretive and ritualistic fraternal order, reflected the anxiety experienced by long-established elites who were now being displaced by new political forces that had greater appeal to the newly enfranchised population. The Masons saw themselves as a bastion of stability in the midst of a society that was being overrun by intemperate rabble. Their existence prompted fear in others, who organized themselves into their own secretive and fraternal orders. Ironically, organizations such as the Guards of Liberty and the Sons of America sprang up to reform those whose behavior was dictated by the very same fears as their own.

Christian evangelism itself suffered nativistic assaults from a small and uninfluential group known as free thinkers, who saw evangelical Christianity as the root of much evil in the nation. Again it must be remembered that the goals and the logic of the feuding forces were similar. Free thinkers were not opposed to the moral principles of Christianity. Rather, they merely thought that such principles needed to be separated from superstitious religious beliefs and grounded in the more scientific laws of nature. One of the leading free-thinker newspapers summed up the group's objections to Christianity when it branded the religious practice as being "mischievous by its false morality; it is mischievous by its hypocrisy; by its fanaticism; by its dogmatism; by its threats; by its hopes; by its promises; and last though not least, by its waste of public time and public money." [36]

Because of their high expectations, the various experiments of the early nineteenth century were destined to fail in the long run as vehicles for myth restoration. Cultural restoration would ultimately depend upon abundance and the opportunity it provided for Americans to once again delude themselves about the future. The approaching age of the machine furnished just such an opportunity.

3.
The Garden of the Machine

By the mid-nineteenth century, anticipation of the golden age of the machine became an important part of America's quest for the kind of Edenic society portrayed in myth. The Civil War briefly interrupted the nation's encounter with the machine age, but when the fighting stopped in 1865, the task of building the ideal industrial state resumed with great vigor.

It is ironic that Americans welcomed industrialization with such open arms because so many of them were critical of its effect on European society a century earlier. From childhood, Americans were taught that Europe was a place of extremes, ranging from the opulence of the aristocracy to the poverty of the working class, a place where callous and greedy industrialists exploited women and children as factory laborers. Europe was portrayed as a place of filthy and crowded cities festering with all manner of human degradation.

These generalizations were reinforced by impressions gained from European critics of industrialization, such as Englishman Thomas Carlyle, who charged that the machine had gained control not only over the material aspects of his society but also over its philosophy, art, and literature. "Men are grown mechanical in head and in heart, as well as in hand. . . . Their whole efforts, attachments, opinions, turn on Mechanism, and are of a mechanical character."[1]

Given the pattern of industrialization that had unfolded in the past and its many undesirable aspects, why did Americans believe that the pattern would be any different in their nation? Certainly part of the answer can be found in the innocence of the New World and in the naive assumption that the evils of Europe could never infiltrate a democratic society. The machine was expected to blend harmoniously into what historian Leo Marx termed a bucolic "middle landscape," which consisted of farms and rolling countryside only occasionally interrupted by small factories quietly nestled in peaceful little villages.[2]

Contrary to Carlyle's charge that industrialization had destroyed England's appreciation of things aesthetic, a fringe element of enthusiastic Americans argued in the 1830s that the machine would enhance rather than diminish achievements in art, literature, and philosophy. The view that Timothy Walker expressed in an 1831 issue of the *North American Review* is typical of what would become in two decades a commonly held view in America. In direct response to Carlyle's concerns, Walker wrote that "the more work we can compel inert matter to do for us, the better will it be for our minds, because the more time shall we have to attend to them." He concluded that as long as people were free, "there would be nothing to hinder all mankind from becoming philosophers, poets, and votaries of art. The whole time and thought of the human race could be given to inward culture and spiritual improvement."[3]

America's endorsement of industrialization was also affected by its ability to convince itself that industrialization would not alter the God-created natural order of things. This was important because Americans based their superiority on being a simple and rustic people, closer to nature and closer to God and thus closer to truth. In an attempt to redefine the natural order of things, enthusiasts argued that people must recognize that they live in a God-created mechanical order and that human happiness rested upon their ability to become knowledgeable of that order. "This world is one of God's workshops," the *Scientific American* reported, and "the universe, a collection of his inventions."[4]

In some quarters the machine was even looked upon as a vehicle through which God's work would be accomplished. It seemed clear to one New England clergyman, for example, that "the village steeple is an unfailing companion to the waterwheel." The machine, for some, was even considered to be an instrument of biblical prophecy. One enthusiast, after viewing a new hay-maker in action, asked, "Are not our inventors absolutely usher-ing in the very dawn of the millennium?"[5]

Indeed, the technological developments of the 1830s and 1840s seem to indicate that American optimism was not without foundation. The nation was dazzled with the introduction of Cyrus McCormick's mechanical reaper (1834), Samuel Colt's revolver (1835), Richard Hoe's rotary printing press (1846), and Elias Howe's sewing machine (1846). Furthermore, the nation was beginning to reap the benefits of the "factory system," a method of manufacturing borrowed from the British. The factory system moved manufacturing from individual households to one central location, where it was coordinated to new levels of efficiency. The textile mills of New England were the first to use the factory system, and it was eventually used in the manufac-ture of watches, firearms, shoes, carpets, and even copper sheets and wire.[6]

The factory system, along with the introduction of inter-changeable parts and steam power, contributed so immensely to American productivity that the value of manufactured goods in the United States increased eightfold between 1812 and the Civil War. Given such miraculous occurrences, it is understandable why the *American Journal of Science* was moved to ask, "What is there yet to be done upon the face of the earth, that cannot be affected by the power of the human mind?"[7]

It appeared as if America would finally be able to fulfill its providentially assigned mission to create a united and harmo-nious world that would reflect the high ideals contained in

American myths. When the trans-Atlantic cable was completed, Samuel Morse wrote that the telegraph would bring about world peace because it would "annihilate space and time" and thus "bring mankind into a common brotherhood." (These same assumptions are found in the futuristic writings about high-tech communication systems, which are discussed in Chapter 5.) Morse's predictions were consistent with those of the *Scientific American* when it concluded that "there is a bright path laid out for our country, that of carrying freedom, science and knowledge to the ends of the earth. May we not neglect to tread in this path of true glory."[8]

Russian serfs were a particularly popular outlet for America's obsession with saving the world. The *Scientific American* spoke optimistically about the consequences that would result from "American mechanics" scattering "the seeds of social freedom in a benighted Russia." One account estimated that twenty-three million serfs owed their freedom to Cyrus McCormick because "with every cut of the McCormick reaper," the *American Artisan* reported, "the shackles of a bondsman of Europe fall clanging to earth!!"[9]

The London Exposition of 1851 and the New York Exposition of 1853 further convinced Americans of their destiny to play a major role in the rejuvenation of the world. The nations of the world gathered at these events to display the essence of their cultural achievements. On these occasions, many noted the stark contrast between the opulent European exhibits and the more utilitarian displays of the United States. Americans were especially struck by the garishness of the Russian exhibit. They gazed upon the "princely magnificence" of the jewels, silks, and furs that were on display. By contrast, they were equally proud that thousands came to see the American exhibit and its display of "water pails made by machinery . . . bell telegraphs and spring chairs and cooking ranges and hot air furnaces and camp bedsteads."[10]

A comparison of the two exhibits confirmed for the Americans that "the Russian exhibit was proof of the wealth, power, enterprise, and intelligence of [Tsar] Nicholas" and that the United States exhibit was "evidence of the ingenuity, industry and capacity of a free and educated people." The Russian exhibit was a "showcase of an emperor to the nobility of Europe," while the U.S. exhibit was an "epistle of a people to the workingmen of the world."[11]

Yet, in spite of the elaborate efforts at self-congratulation, there were strong indications that Americans continued to suffer from an inferiority complex in matters of art and literature. They went to great lengths to explain to the world and to convince themselves that they were not a crude people lacking in aesthetic appreciation. They argued that "inventions are the poetry of the physical science and the inventors, the poets." The *Scientific American* pondered, "Who can tell of the dreamings — the wakeful nightly dreams of inventors, their abstractions and enthusiastic reveries to create some ballad or produce some epic in machinery?" With the invention of the steamer, these "bards of machinery" had created "a mightier epic than the *Iliad* — and Whitney, Jackquard and Blanchard might laugh even Virgil, Milton and Tasso to scorn." These achievements, in the minds of some American enthusiasts, elevated their culture far beyond what heretofore had been defined as refined culture. "The workshops of Watt and Fulton, Bell and Stevenson, have turned the world upside down by their inventions, while sages of Oxford and Cambridge have but added some new theorems to the Principia." Few in America would have disagreed with the *Scientific American* when it concluded that "it is a happy privilege we enjoy of living in an age, which for its inventions and discoveries, its improvements in intelligence and virtue stands without rival in the history of the world."[12]

By the 1850s enthusiasm for the machines had moved from the pages of esoteric scientific and technological journals into the everyday consciousness of Americans. Europeans were struck by America's obsession with machinery. A Swedish novelist commented that when American schoolchildren were allowed to draw on their slates for recreation, they almost always drew "smoking steam-engines, or steamboats, all in movement." A French observer, Michael Chevalier, noted the American had a "perfect passion for railroads; he loves them . . . as a lover loves his mistress." Another noted that "the railroad, animated by its powerful locomotive, appears to be the characteristic personification of the American. The one seems to hear and understand the other . . . to have been made for the other . . . to be indispensable to the other."[13]

Northerners boldly charged into the late nineteenth century confident that the defeat of the South had removed the last remaining obstacle to industrial progress. Americans had every reason to feel confident. The signs of progress were everywhere. The parade of inventions begun by McCormick, Eli Whitney, Howe, and others before the Civil War was continued in the dazzling array of post–Civil War technological innovations, such as Alexander Bell's telephone (1876) and Thomas Edison's incandescent light bulb (1879).[14]

Meanwhile, Francis Bowen's influential economic text counseled national leaders to let nature take its course. "Leave the course of trade and the condition of society alone," he wrote, because when "God regulates things, by His general laws they always in the long run work to the good." Indeed it appeared that Bowen was right. Everywhere one looked, economic expansion had become the password to progress. By the turn of the century, America could boast of having the most rapidly growing economy in the world. The excitement of the period was beautifully captured by an English visitor in 1900 when he described the United States as "one perpetual swirl of telephones, telegrams, phonographs, electric bells, motors, lifts and automatic instruments." Unfortunately, the "perpetual swirl" of events also meant that Americans would be challenged by circumstances that came upon them so quickly that it would be impossible for them to fully grasp their meaning.[15]

DISILLUSIONMENT

By the turn of the century, it was obvious that the emerging industrial order was proving to be yet another threat to key national myths. Farmers and industrialists were among the first to experience the consequences of unregulated industrial expansion. Urbanization had led to expanded agricultural and industrial markets, and bankers and merchants, eager to take advantage of these boom conditions, freely extended credit to farmers who thought that their success was tied to the increased production that would result from owning more land and more modern equipment. By the turn of the century, nine hundred corporations were busily manufacturing $92 million worth of steam-powered tractors, combines, threshers, and an assortment of other farm implements. In the twenty years between 1870 and 1890, the amount of wheat harvested increased from 254 million bushels to 1 billion bushels, and the amount of corn, hay, and cotton produced more than doubled.[16]

Unfortunately, farmers failed to realize until it was too late that increased production created surpluses that lowered prices and diminished profits. Farmers, ignorant of the reality of such conditions, continued to use credit with reckless abandon to purchase more equipment and more land in order to make up for the decline in commodity prices. In the end, this practice resulted in even lower prices for their crops. Thus, farmers were caught in an endless debt cycle and in a depressing malaise over their inability to control the marketplace and, by implication, their inability to control their own personal destinies, as they had been acculturated to believe they could.[17]

The emerging industrial order presented businesspeople with a similar set of economic challenges. Industrialists, like farmers, had the capability to produce more goods, which in turn led to lower prices and lower profit margins. Industrialists, however, were more successful than farmers in responding to these challenges. They countered lower profit margins by lowering wages and effectively using advertising to stimulate greater consumption of their products. Most important, they attempted to eliminate competition through consolidation. During the last decade of the nineteenth century and the early years of the twentieth century, businesses were merged under trust and holding company arrangements in unprecedented numbers. In 1899 alone, 1,028 companies were swallowed up by larger business units. U.S. Steel took control of 170 firms in that year and in the process gained control over 65 percent of the market. At the same time, American Tobacco absorbed 162 firms and subsequently was able to capture 90 percent of the market. Furthermore, by the turn of the century, over a thousand railroad lines were consolidated into six major systems. Giant corporations, such as Standard Oil, U.S. Steel, American Tobacco, E. I. Dupont, American Can, National Biscuit Company, International Harvester, Borden Foods, General Electric, and Westinghouse, were the victors in the colossal struggle for the spoils of the industrial state. By 1904 holding companies controlled 40 percent of the nation's industries.[18]

The heart and soul of America's rise to industrial preeminence was the city. In addition to acting as the hub of the new industrial order, the city was the symbol of modernity. If it was urban, it was up-to-date. Cities were thought to offer excitement, variety, adventure, and escape from the ordinary. The promise of the city lured rural Americans as well as foreign immigrants in such great numbers that by 1900 approximately one-third of the nation's citizens lived in cities of at least eight thousand people.[19]

Foreign immigrants contributed greatly to urban growth in America. By the end of World War I, 38.4 percent of the population, or more than one out of every three Americans, were considered to be immigrants, and 75 percent of them were crowded into the cities. Most of those who came to the cities with such high expectations were sadly disillusioned by what they found. The limited resources of the immigrants forced them to live in crowded and unsanitary tenement houses. These buildings, often windowless and without ventilation, were the source of countless horror stories.[20]

Frederick Lewis Allen, a noted chronicler of this time, observed that to read accounts of the living and working conditions of these people "is to hear variation after variation upon the theme of human misery, in which the same words occur monotonously again and again: wretchedness, overcrowding, filth, hunger, malnutrition, insecurity, want." Robert Hunter's famous book on poverty in 1904 recorded that "heavy brooding men; tired, anxious women; thinly dressed, unkempt little girls; and frail, joyless lads passed along, half awake, not one utters a word as they hurried to the great factory." He witnessed workers with "hunger-hollowed faces" and "shoulders narrowed with consumption, girls of fifteen as old as grandmothers, who had never eaten a bit of meat in their lives."[21]

An 1899 report on the condition of Boston tenements found "dirty and battered walls and ceilings, dark cellars with water standing in them, alleys littered with garbage and filth, broken and leaking drain pipes . . . dark and filthy water-closets long frozen or otherwise out of order . . . and houses so dilapidated and so much settled that they are dangerous." Jacob Riis, a vocal critic of slum landlords in New York City, spoke of visiting houses in which "the beams are rotten and alive with vermin." The health department in New York reported that in "66 old houses, with a population of 5460 tenants . . . there had been 1313 deaths in a little over five years [1889–1894]."[22]

The majority of the white, native-born Americans, however, did not suffer the plight of the immigrant. Until the depression of 1893, these people continued to be optimistic about the future even though the nation's problems, especially urban degradation, were becoming more visible. The living standard of most white, Anglo-Saxon Protestants improved through the 1880s. One out of every five Americans moved from blue-collar into white-collar jobs during this time, and unskilled laborers moved into skilled or semiskilled positions at the same rate. Given these circumstances, it was easy to argue that the degradation of the cities was directly related to the inferiority of the southern and eastern Europeans who lived there. As long as Americans could rationalize in this manner, the myths surrounding opportunity and freedom were not in immediate danger. All of this changed, however, with the devastating depression of 1893. This depression was so severe that it even affected more established, "old stock" Americans. Consequently, it became more and more difficult to explain failure in terms of nationality or genetic makeup.

EXPERIMENTATION AND MYTH RESTORATION

By the late nineteenth century, America became what historian Robert Wiebe has called "a society without a core."[23] Once again rapid change and newness had threatened egalitarian and individualistically based national myths, which were the key to societal stability. Industrialization made it difficult for Americans to continue to be optimistic about the future. There is a rich body of literature on the Progressive period in American history; it is not the purpose of this inquiry to delve yet again into political reform in the early twentieth century. The focus here, as in the first cycle of myth restoration, will be on education, health, diet, and exercise, as well as on pseudoscience and nativism, as therapeutic aids in helping individuals cope with change and in realigning themselves with the illusive American dream.

As in the first cycle of myth restoration, some Americans sought to stop the perceived erosion of equality and opportunity through educational reform. Pragmatism and its originator, William James, and "progressive" education and its leading proponent,

John Dewey, were vital factors in the reorientation of educational thinking. Even though the circumstances that had caused the perceived need for educational reform had changed, the reformers of the early twentieth century did not differ significantly from their early nineteenth-century counterparts on two key points. First, both generations of educational reformers saw a close link between the development of a true democracy in America and the level of education of its citizens. Horace Mann, for example, would not have disagreed with Dewey's assumption that "a government resting upon popular suffrage cannot be successful unless those who elect and who obey their governors are educated." Second, both generations of educational reformers saw the fulfillment of America's promise in terms of individual behavior modification rather than through systemic change.[24]

Industrialization and the emergence of Darwinian science were the most serious obstacles to the continuation of American beliefs about equality, opportunity, and, ultimately, the restoration of a democratic way of life. Darwinian science, with its implicit determinism — its portrayal of living things as pawns of the forces of nature — threatened individualism and the cherished belief that one must be able to control one's own destiny in a democracy.

It is quite obvious that change had once again come so rapidly and in such strange forms that it was difficult to find stability in any one set of beliefs. John Dewey reflects this concern when he noted that "a society which is mobile, which is full of channels for the distribution of a change occurring anywhere, must see to it that its members are educated to personal initiative and adaptability. Otherwise they will be overwhelmed by the changes in which they are caught and whose significance or connections they do not perceive." [25]

Noted philosopher William James reflected the same anxiety when he expressed his concern about the often times bad habits that are oftentimes established in the early years of human development. "Could the young but realize," he wrote, "how soon they will become mere walking bundles of habits, they would give more heed to their conduct while in the plastic state. We are spinning our fates, good or evil, and never to be undone." According to James, it was impossible for humans to react intelligently to change because their actions were inextricably tied to deep-seated notions that had little bearing on present reality. He argued that people must recognize that "the truth of an idea is not a stagnant property inherent in it." He insisted that "truth happens to an idea. It becomes true, is made true by events. Its verity is in fact an event, a process: the process namely of its verifying itself, its veri-fication." In other words, consistent with the myth of free agency, truth is what one says it is.[26]

It was John Dewey who, in *The School and Society* (1899), formalized "progressive" education. His role was to incorporate the relativism of James with pedagogical experiments in education already under way in America. Dewey believed that industrialization had a negative impact on American society. Industrialization and the rapid change it fostered rendered traditional forms of education, based on absolute truth and rote learning, useless. "If our education is to have any meaning for life," Dewey wrote, "it must pass through an equally complete transformation." The transformation Dewey had in mind focused on learning principles through hands-on experience. He observed that children living in an agrarian environment were more actively involved in the economic life of the family and more closely associated with the real, practical world. He argued that this form of training for the young had vanished in industrial America. Thus, according to Dewey, schools needed to strive to recreate an atmosphere in which the traditional emphasis on static truths would be deemphasized in favor of an educational environment in which the child's natural creativity would be unleashed. Students should learn to read and write through daily interaction with one another and by writing their own material rather than relying on standard textbooks. Students should learn science from actual experiences, such as growing crops on the school's grounds.[27]

Educators were so receptive to Dewey's reasoning that it would become the philosophy of American education until well after World War II. Consistent with Dewey's philosophy, educators placed greater emphasis on training children to think for themselves and at the same time emphasized a more practical vocational education. In retrospect it could be argued that James and Dewey made it possible for Americans to abandon past beliefs more comfortably and to move into the future without fearing that change would destroy their way of life. In addition, the relativism contained in the philosophy of pragmatism allowed educators to continue to believe in free agency and self-reliance without abandoning compelling arguments on the importance of the environment in shaping human affairs.

As was the case in the first cycle of myth restoration, greater public awareness was a byproduct of widespread anxiety. Americans at the dawn of the twentieth century were once again faced with unacceptable levels of political corruption, poverty, alcohol and drug abuse, and the dangerous side effects of the fast-paced life-style of the industrial order. Historians are well aware of the role that muckraking journalists played in focusing America's attention on political corruption and on unethical business practices. However, historians have not recognized the role that muckraking journalism played in reaffirming national myths. It could be argued that when muckrakers revealed that greedy and powerful individuals were the cause of economic inequality and social injustice, they at the same time revealed that America's problems were not the fault of the system itself and by implication not the fault of its underlying myths. [28]

Another form of education was to be found in the vast array of self-help books that provided hope that economic success was still possible in America. In addition to the popular Horatio Alger stories, there was Orison Swett Marden's *Pushing to the Front,* which ran through 250 editions, and Samuel Smiles's popular series, which contained titles such as *Self Help, Character, Thrift,* and *Duty.* These books offered the hope to their readers that opportunities still existed for those who worked hard and persevered despite temporary adversity. The individualistic message of these books matched the self-focused perspective of the average reader. This made it easy for these readers to continue to believe that they were the exception to what was happening to millions of other Americans and that they could succeed in spite of the odds against them.

The Chautauqua movement was another educational vehicle, albeit an informal one, though which the public gained a greater awareness of national problems and prescriptions for dealing with them. First organized in 1874, by 1900 the Chautauqua movement had expanded into thirty-one states and was publishing its own books and its own slick magazine called the *Chautauquan.* Although its primary role was entertainment, the Chautauqua movement was also an important educational forum. Some of its speakers provided useful information on a wide range of topics to audiences that otherwise did not have access to such knowledge. The Chautauqua movement, however, also provided a platform for health and diet hucksters to peddle their wares and for those who preached the gospel of nativism. It could be argued that the Chautauqua movement served the same function in myth restoration as did the lyceum of the early nineteenth century and myriad television talk shows today. It satisfied the needs of an anxious public eager to believe anyone or anything that might restore their faith in America.[29]

Public awareness of alcohol and drug abuse and even of the dangers of the fast-paced life-style of the late nineteenth and early twentieth centuries reached peak levels. Almost every sector of American society was exposed to lectures about the dangers of alcohol. Conservative Christians were told that alcohol abuse was a clear sign of a sinful soul, while modernist Christians saw consumption of the substance as an ugly consequence of the overall debilitating environment of the new industrial order. Meanwhile, the scientific community presented evidence that refuted long-standing beliefs about the substance. For the first time it was revealed that alcohol depressed rather than stimulated memory, judgment, and motor control. Soon, lay versions of such findings began to appear in popular magazines, making the public even more aware of the dangers of alcohol.[30]

Businesspeople, labor leaders, and government agencies, such as the National Council of Safety, were also a part of the antiliquor crusade. An impressive array of statistics was presented to the public to support the contention that a dry workplace had a competitive advantage over those that were wet. In West Virginia, for example, it was reported that Prohibition had increased the output of coal per man from 908 tons in 1914 to 964 tons in 1915. Furthermore, a survey covering eighteen medium-sized cities reported that Prohibition had led to "an increase in bank deposits," and it "stimulated retail trade, improved collections, and greatly increased attendance at amusement parks."[31]

The fast pace of industrial living and its association with mental illness and with the use of harmful narcotics was another popular concern of Americans. One observer noted that "we live too fast; we do as much in a day as our forefathers did in a week, and physically, we are not so well qualified for work as they were. We eat too fast; we think and read and even take our recreation at a high rate of speed." Indeed these charges were not totally without foundation. In the early twentieth century, doctors reported an unprecedented number of cases of neurasthenia, or nervous exhaustion.[32]

In 1881 George Beard, a recognized expert on nervous disorders, warned that Americans were "essentially a nervous people, prone to go to excess in everything, gladly welcoming narcotics and stimulants." Current research indicates that Beard's observations were remarkably accurate. Historian H. Wayne Morgan, in his study on drugs in America, indicated that while the population of the United States grew 83 percent between 1880 and 1910, the sale of patent medicines grew 700 percent. Unfortunately, many of these patent medicines contained opium, morphine, cocaine, or any one of a variety of other addictive substances.[33]

The nation eventually did become aware of its growing drug addiction problem. In 1902 a committee of pharmacists estimated that there were two hundred thousand addicts in the country. Sixteen years later a U.S. Treasury Department committee placed the number at one million. To combat the problem, the medical profession in 1898 turned to a new miracle drug known as heroin. Heroin was thought to be nonaddictive because it was taken intravenously, and it was a well-established fact that drugs taken in this manner could not become addictive. Heroin even received a qualified endorsement from the American Medical Association's Council on Pharmacy and Chemistry.[34]

For some, physiological redemption was the answer to the problems confronting America at the turn of the century. As in the early nineteenth century, health, diet, and exercise regimens had appeal to an individualistic citizenry eager to find the competitive edge and to unlock the secrets of success. Health evangelists, such as Horace Fletcher and John Kellogg, like Sylvester Graham in the previous century, provided therapeutic relief to their followers because they gave plausible explanations for failure and a precisely defined prescription for success.

Fletcher saw many of the nation's failings in terms of the improper ingestion of food, which he thought was the result of the fast pace of industrial living. Fletcher preached that efficient levels of food ingestion could be achieved by thoroughly chewing or masticating one's food. He was convinced that proper ingestion resulted in the body's making more efficient use of the nutritional value that food had to offer. Greater ingestive efficiency, according to Fletcher, meant that the body would need fewer calories, especially those associated with protein, which was considered to be the cause of many diseases.[35]

Fletcher's books and lectures attracted thousands of follow-ers. Some were fortunate enough to visit John Kellogg's sanato-rium in Battle Creek, Michigan. Kellogg, a Fletcher enthusiast, was also convinced of the evils of protein, especially that which was contained in red meat. In his book *Shall We Slay to Eat,* he labeled meat as the greatest enemy to good health and, by implication, the cause of many of the nation's failings. The danger, according to Kellogg, was the diseases caused by the bacteria that formed on the undigested meat that was left in the colon. He described this as being "fairly alive and swarming with the identical micro-organisms found in a dead rat in a closet or the putrefying carcass of a cow in barnyard filth."[36]

Kellogg eventually incorporated mastication, or "Fletcher-izing" as he called it, into the daily regimen for his sanatorium patients. He even composed a chewing song to help his patients pass the time through the arduous chewing ordeal. Notables such as President William Howard Taft, John D. Rockefeller, Jr., Alfred Du Pont, J. C. Penney, Montgomery Ward, and Edgar Welch all traveled to Battle Creek to sing and chew their way to a rejuve-nated life. It has been estimated that "the San," as it was popularly known, treated over three hundred thousand people between 1876 and the time of Kellogg's death in 1943.[37]

Of course, most Americans were not die-hard disciples of Horace Fletcher, nor were they aware of Kellogg's sanatorium. Yet it can be said that the majority of Americans were more health conscious during this period than in the past. Popular magazines such as the *Ladies Home Journal* instructed the public to ignore the eating habits of bygone times. "Read the cook-books of great-great grandmother's day — and marvel!" it admonished. "Plenty of rich, heavy food for every meal. . . . Her family survived it is true. They ate at her groaning board and got away with it. But life was different then." Accordingly, Americans were inundated with advice on how to change their eating habits to meet the needs of "the strain, the sedentary work and the nervous intensity of modern living."[38]

To assist them in their quest for physiological renewal, Americans were presented with newly created "health foods," such as canned soups and dry breakfast cereals. The advertisements for these products clearly indicated that their appeal rested upon their promise to give individuals a competitive edge in the race for the material spoils of the tattered industrial Eden. A *Saturday Evening Post* advertisement for Post Bran Flakes even went so far as to incorporate the "survival of the fittest" message of social Darwinism. It contrasted a weary and haggard-looking businessman, who was obviously having difficulty coping with the rigors of cutthroat competition, with another businessman who was neat, tidy, and who appeared to be well on his way to achieving the kind of success that people were taught to expect in the land of opportunity. The advertisement's copy, meanwhile, suggested that proper bowel movement was critical to those who hoped to emerge victorious in the struggle and that Post Bran Flakes was the sure prescription for both proper bowel movement and the success that would follow.[39]

Americans were also inundated with health-oriented books offering renewed hope that a prosperous and fulfilling life was more than mere fantasy. Bernarr MacFadden became a multimillionaire publishing books with titles such as *Hair Culture, Strengthening the Spine, Foot Troubles,* and his massive, five-volume *Encyclopedia of Physical Culture.* Reaffirming the myth of free agency, MacFadden wrote: "The healthy person is unconscious of discomfort . . . he rises superior to it — is absolutely the monarch of all he surveys. He dominates life instead of allowing it to dominate him."[40]

Americans' sudden increase in enthusiasm for diet was matched only by their enthusiasm for exercise. Exercise, to the devoted, was perceived not only as a cure for a host of diseases but also as an antidote for many of the nation's social and economic problems. Exercise, according to one publication, gave "energy and daring a legitimate channel." It took the "place of war, gambling, licentiousness, high-way robbery and officeseeking. . . .

It gives an innocent answer to that first demand for evening excitement which perils the soul of the homeless boy in the seductive city." It was the "only thorough panacea" that made "the whole voyage of life self-curative." Even the usually staid and sedentary business community got caught up in the exercise mania. For example, it was not uncommon to witness office workers standing next to their desks while being led in a daily exercise routine.[41]

Bicycling was the most popular mode of exercise in the early twentieth century. The bicycle was portrayed in medical journals and popular magazines as a medical "preparation of steel and rubber . . . far more beneficent in its health and life giving than all the pills and potions ever invented." Bicycling was an activity that had advanced the race a "hundred years." Another source proclaimed that "the bicycle has done more for the good of the human race than all the medicines compounded since the days of Hippocrates. . . . It seems hard to believe, but we feel that the doctor's occupation is gone." In addition to its beneficial effect in dyspepsia, anemia, obesity, curvature of the spine, asthma, varicose veins, heart disease, and diabetes, bicycling was believed to be a cure for drug abuse, alcoholism, and smoking. The pedaling mania was even credited with reducing the consumption of cigars in 1896 by one million per day.[42]

Moses Coit Tyler, the noted educator and historian, even insisted that religion and health were interrelated and indistinguishable from one another. He argued that the Bible offered compelling proof that sickness was the equivalent of sin. Tyler argued that the Bible "says that since every part of our nature is the sacred gift of God, he who neglects his body . . . who allows it to grow up puny, frail, sickly, mis-shapen, homely, commits a sin against the giver of the body."[43]

Unfortunately, anxiety once again led to extreme expressions of nativism, with their odious logic that the nation's problems were the result of the presence of unacceptable races and ethnic groups. As in the past, the practice of blaming national problems on immigrants was sanctioned by some educators, scientists, and even theologians. For some, social Darwinism provided compelling evidence that the unfit should be scorned. Herbert Spencer used Darwin's theories, especially the notion of the survival of the fittest, to argue that human progress was made possible by the fit, who reigned supreme in the struggle to survive. He concluded, therefore, that those who assisted the weak were doing the nation a disservice because they were impeding human progress.[44]

In scientific circles, the study of eugenics gave racism and nativism a further degree of legitimacy. Eugenics, an early science of genetics that reached peak popularity between 1905 and 1930, was based upon the principle that heredity was the most important factor in determining behavior. One early leader in the eugenics movement defined it as "the science of the improvement of the human race by better breeding." Historian Mark Haller wrote that during this period many scientists came to believe that "most feeblemindedness and a good proportion of insanity, crime, and pauperism lay in heredity." Haller found that their conviction was so strong and shared by so many that it led to the sterilization of "defective" types in "virtually every state." The fascination with genetic manipulation today has once again taken center stage in some scientific circles and for some is the basis for renewed Edenic projections for the future. Unfortunately, it could also become the basis for a renewed form of the kind of discrimination that is often found in extreme types of nativism.[45]

Best-selling books such as Madison Grant's *The Passing of the Great Race* (1918) and Lothrop Stoddard's *The Rising Tide of Color* (1920), also contributed to nativistic hysteria. Grant warned an already anxious public that the flood of immigrants who had come to America were jeopardizing not only the nation's superiority but ultimately its very existence. According to Grant, the fall of white civilization was imminent because these "immigrant laborers are now breeding out their masters and killing by filth and by crowding as effectively as by the sword."[46]

Stoddard warned that the "white stock" in the western part of the United States was being "swamped" by inferior Asiatic blood. According to Stoddard, Anglo-Saxon superiority was responsible for its own undoing because "the white man's very triumphs have evoked this danger. . . . His virtual abolition of distance has destroyed the protection which nature once conferred." The only solution, according to Stoddard, was to erect "artificial barriers" for future immigration. He indicated that if this was not done, the "various races will increasingly mingle and the inevitable result will be the supplanting or abortion of the higher by the lower types."[47]

Another form of nativistic paranoia, the "red scare," was created by the Bolshevik Revolution of 1917. The occurrence of the communist takeover in Russia at the same time that the United States was experiencing high levels of unemployment and labor unrest following World War I caused many Americans to believe that the two were directly related. Attorney General A. Mitchell Palmer warned that communism was "eating its way into the home of the American workman, its sharp tongue of revolutionary heat . . . licking the altars of churches, leaping into the belfry of the school bell, crawling into the sacred corners of the American home, burning up the foundation of society." These fears eventually resulted in the creation of the Federal Bureau of Investigation (FBI). This agency, led by J. Edgar Hoover, was charged with rooting out the odious radicals who were infesting the land of freedom and opportunity.[48]

Blacks also suffered from the nativistic hysteria of that time. Beginning in the 1880s, rural southern blacks came to northern urban industrial centers to fulfill their expectations of the American dream. Opportunities seemed especially great during World War I because of the large number of white laborers who were called off to war. Blacks quickly learned, however, that life in the

North was filled with the same lack of opportunity and the same racism that they had faced in the South. A renewed round of negrophobia among whites and the frustration of blacks, especially in the urban North, culminated in a series of urban race riots in 1919. Blacks, displaying a new militancy as espoused by the NAACP (National Association for the Advancement of Colored People), which was organized a decade earlier, fought off attacking white mobs in both the North and the South. These riots were a reminder to nativistically inclined whites that the American way of life was being threatened not only from external radical forces but also from within their own society.

Such fears explain why groups who saw themselves as self-appointed protectors of the American way of life were once again so popular. For example, the infamous Ku Klux Klan thrived during this period, claiming to have five million members from all walks of life.[49] Ironically, the goal of the Klan, and of other nativistic groups as well, differed little from that of the more liberal political and social reformers. In its own distorted way, the Klan was also seeking to restore the opportunity and freedom portrayed in the nation's most cherished myths.

In every sector of society in the late nineteenth and early twentieth centuries, America lacked cohesiveness. Walter Lippmann described the nation best when he wrote: "We are unsettled to the very roots of our being. . . . There are no precedents to guide us, no wisdom that wasn't for a simpler age."[50] Unknown to Lippmann and his fellow Americans, they were already being prepared for yet another escape into the future. This time the principles of scientific management would be looked upon as the savior of the nation.

4.
The Eden of the Expert: Scientific Management and Bureaucracies

Some Americans were able to weather the crisis created by unregulated industrialization in the late nineteenth century because they found short-term therapeutic relief in the various political, social, and economic experiments undertaken at the time. These experiments were unwittingly a part of the growing enthusiasm for planning and efficiency as the way to achieve a societal order that at last would contain a responsible free citizenry, competing fairly for the riches of America.

In addition, journalists and a cadre of academics in a variety of fields contributed to myth restoration by making it appear as if there was nothing inherently wrong with the nation and the principles by which it conducted its affairs. More specifically, the intelligentsia was able to convince most Americans that the nation's problems were the direct result of a few greedy and powerful industrialists and bankers who had managed to frustrate the natural order of the free enterprise system.

The intelligentsia not only identified the culprits but also provided the prescription for building a true land of opportunity. Scientific management, according to the leading minds in America, would at last usher in a golden age of freedom, opportunity, equality, and spiritual fulfillment. Where others had failed, it was assumed that professionally trained management experts

functioning within a strong central government would be successful in achieving the idyllic goal because they would be
indifferent to special-interest groups and would thus serve as a
check against the powerful and selfish forces that had corrupted
the system in the past.

Henry George and Edward Bellamy were the most notable
of the early enthusiasts who had endorsed the concept of a strong
central government. George's solution was simple and straight-
forward. In his famous book, *Progress and Poverty* (1879), he
proposed that a "single tax be levied on those who derived profit
from the rent of property which they owned but did not actually
work themselves." George was convinced that this tax, when
administered by a strong central government, would eliminate
the need for all other forms of taxation. He felt that this would
relieve common laborers from the burden of taxation and provide
them with a greater opportunity to succeed. Edward Bellamy took
a similar approach in *Looking Backward* (1887), a fictional piece
that depicted a utopian society in the year A.D. 2000. Bellamy's
America of the future was ruled by a strong central government,
and impartial experts with a wide range of power were depicted
as being managers of a system that all but ran itself.[1]

George and Bellamy were not alone in singing the praises
of a planned, centralized state. A large number of social scientists
in the early twentieth century tinkered with the idea of achieving
a more equitable society. In the late nineteenth century, there
were a number of young economists who had received their
training in German universities and were thus strongly influ-
enced by the centralized German state established under the rule
of Otto von Bismarck. One of these, Richard Ely, joined with other
like-minded scholars in 1885 to form the American Economic
Association, an organization dedicated to building a similar Bis-
marckian society in America. Ely and his colleagues believed that
conflicts between "labor and capital" were responsible for a "vast
number of social problems." They felt that if scientific methods,
rather than mere speculation, were employed to understand and

manage the "the actual conditions of economic life," a more harmonious and peaceful society would be the result. Ely and his colleagues, however, insisted that these goals could only be accomplished if the nation was ruled by a strong central government that was actively involved in the economic affairs of its citizens.[2]

Herbert Croly provided the most comprehensive and most brilliant rationalizations for the establishment of a strong central government. The problems of the late nineteenth and early twentieth centuries, according to Croly, were the result of conditions that had frustrated the achievement of two goals: individual liberty and the public good. Croly argued that the "unfettered individualism" that people enjoyed in the pursuit of profit prior to the Civil War had only resulted in injustices in the industrial state that developed following that war. "The plain fact is," wrote Croly in his opus, *The Promise of American Life* (1909), "that the individual in freely and energetically pursuing his own private purposes has not been the inevitable public benefactor assumed by the traditional American interpretation of democracy." According to Croly, the weak central government of the earlier period had allowed "unusually energetic and unscrupulous men" to seize too much power. Under these circumstances, freedom and "practically unrestricted economic opportunities are precisely the condition which makes for bondage."[3]

Ironically, while consolidation in business was seen as a major threat to democracy, consolidation in matters of government was considered to be the savior of democracy. According to Croly, the true restoration of democracy could only happen under the auspices of a strong central government controlled by experts. Such a government was the key to the "promise of individual moral and intellectual emancipation," because it would have the power to intervene in the affairs of society and thus create a more equitable society. Croly argued that in order for citizens to have true freedom they must relinquish the kind of freedom associated with the "unfettered individualism" of the

early nineteenth century. In *The Promise of American Life,* Croly
managed brilliantly to merge the myths of free agency and the
land of opportunity with newer realities that called for a more
regulated society. He did so without being consciously aware of
any of the contradictions that might have existed in his logic.[4]

The average American, of course, was not conversant with
the arguments presented by the intelligentsia extolling the virtues of scientific management. The masses, however, were eventually introduced to scientific management as a result of
Frederick Taylor's success in making factory production more
efficient. Beginning in the 1880s, Taylor gained a reputation for
dramatically increasing production in a number of factories by
increasing the efficiency of the work force. The infamous factory
assembly line was born out of Taylor's method of breaking down
larger jobs into smaller segments. He used a stopwatch to time
the movements of workers in relation to their machines with an
eye toward eliminating wasted motion. Time standards were
established for each individual task, and workers were paid on a
piecework basis. Finally, professional managers were employed
to coordinate these seemingly meaningless tasks into a comprehensive production scheme. The Taylor system, however, did
more than merely increase industrial production. As a result of
the piecework method of pay, the system unwittingly preserved
the ability of workers, or so it was thought, to control their own
destinies.[5]

Popular magazines and newspapers made Taylor's principles of scientific management so popular in the early years of
the twentieth century that they were soon applied to almost
every task in American society. Americans were confident that
they had at last found a way in which to create the kind of society
that conformed to their self-image. Except for the federal government, according to historian Otis Graham, "state and local gov-
ernments, corporations, universities, churches, and other
private institutions continued to centralize their activities, to add
research and operating agencies specialized by function, and to

move toward standardized procedures, all designed to extend control over unpredictable environments."[6]

Even the church was viewed as a theological factory and expected to conduct its business according to the principles of efficient factory management. As one minister put it, "People like to be tied up to progressive, wide awake and going concerns." Bruce Barton's best-seller, *The Man That Nobody Knows,* described Jesus Christ as the ultimate efficiency expert because He "picked up twelve men from the bottom ranks of business and forged them into an organization that conquered the world." Books and articles with intriguing titles such as "Efficiency in Church Work," "Organizing the Church for Efficient Economic Service," *Scientific Management in the Churches,* and *The Principles of Church Advertising* are a further indication of the pervasiveness of Taylor's influence.[7]

Homemaking was another of the unlikely areas in American society in which scientific management made itself felt. Mary Pattison's popular book, *The Business of Home Management: The Principles of Domestic Engineering,* was joined by magazine articles with revealing titles such as "The Waste of Private Housekeeping," "Household Engineering: Scientific Management in the Home," "A Brandeis for the Kitchen," "Scientific Management in the Family," and "Increasing Household Efficiency." Women were told that the home was "part of the great factory for the production of citizens." One efficiency expert pronounced that "our hope is to bring the masculine and feminine mind more closely together in the industry of home-making by raising housework to the plane of Scientific Engineering." The *Ladies Home Journal,* after running a series of articles on the subject, received sixteen hundred letters from readers requesting more information.[8]

The severe trauma of the Great Depression of the 1930s created a unique opportunity for the implementation of many of the idealistic government schemes that the intelligentsia had fashioned earlier in the century. It was a time when managerial and technical experts were given more authority to effect change than ever before. Unfortunately, while the machinery for planning and control was in place, the mind-set of those operating that machinery was inextricably tied to the same set of myths that had been dictating American behavior all along. Their efforts were still directed toward enhancing the competitiveness of the average American with the assumption that ethics and equality would take care of themselves if citizens were only given a fair change.

Indeed, on the surface it appeared as if the programs of the New Deal were fulfilling the great expectations held out for the centralized Eden of the expert. By 1940 the federal government employed over one million people as compared with approximately thirty-seven thousand on the eve of the Civil War. According to Otis Graham, the federal government had assumed regulatory powers over "agriculture, banking, labor-management relations, resource use, radio broadcasting, food and drug quality, aviation, the wages and hours of labor in interstate commerce." It loaned money to "farmers and homeowners, railroads and banks; was producing and selling electricity, dispensing pensions to the aged, relief to the unemployed, and devising employment for destitute artists, architects, city planners, and novelists."[9]

DISILLUSIONMENT

The bureaucracy of the New Deal was in reality a tangled snarl of agencies, many of whose responsibilities overlapped. Under these circumstances, agencies often found themselves in competition with one another and were thus forced to jealously guard their powers from being usurped. The federal government, as imposing as it may have appeared on the surface, was forced to carefully zigzag a course between competing interest groups that continued to command an inordinate amount of power. Its tax measures, according to Graham, accomplished "none of the goals announced for it such as the prevention of monopoly or redistribution of income or wealth." Despite its seeming boldness, the New Deal represented only a mild departure from the interest group–dominated society that it had inherited.[10]

Clearly, the political, economic, and social order that emerged during the New Deal was neither the free-enterprise system envisioned in the early nineteenth century nor the scientifically planned society envisioned by Ely, Croly, and others at the beginning of the twentieth century. The government did not take exclusive control over society, rather it shared power with those interest groups that were strong enough to exert significant influence on public policy. By the mid-1950s there were already signs of disillusionment among the intelligentsia of the nation. Sociologist David Riesman, businessman William Whyte, and social commentators such as Paul Goodman were but a few of those who severely criticized the America of the 1950s. In doing so they were unwittingly showing their frustration over the gap that existed between innocent American myths and the reality that surrounded them.

Riesman was especially troubled by the inability of Americans to think for themselves. In *The Lonely Crowd* (1950), he argued that Americans had changed from being "inner directed" to being "other directed." He argued that prior to industrialization, the "inner directed" Americans still possessed the bold pioneering spirit that had allowed them to blaze new paths without fearing the consequences of their actions. Territories were settled and the foundations for great industries were laid as a result of this strong and independent spirit. By contrast, the product of the regimented order of the day, "other directed" Americans, had neither the inclination nor the will to think for themselves, preferring to look to others for direction and approval.[11]

William Whyte, a leading businessman and former editor of *Fortune* magazine, told much the same story in his noted work *The Organization Man* (1956). He reported that a disturbing "new social ethic" was emerging in American business that he felt had frustrated individualism because it had placed a premium on the group as a source of "creativity," making "belongingess" the ultimate need of the individual. Even more depressing, these businesspeople appeared to be totally unaware of their conformity consciousness. According to Whyte, they had constructed "what would be seen in other times as a bill of no rights into a restatement of individualism." Others were more direct in their criticism. Paul Goodman wrote that America had become a nation that "thwarts aptitude and creates stupidity. It corrupts ingenious patriotism. It corrupts the fine arts. It shackles science. It dampens animal ardor. . . . It has no honor. It has no community." To the discerning eye, Goodman's statement, as crude as it is, nicely summarizes the themes of disillusionment that date back to the early nineteenth century.[12]

As the 1950s wore on, criticisms of the organizational society and its rigid structures and conformity consciousness became more visible because of the rhetoric and life-style of the beat generation. Beat writers, such as Jack Kerouac and Allen Ginsberg, expressed many of the same concerns that troubled the intelligentsia but in a manner that attracted a great deal more attention. Allen Ginsberg's poetry struck out at an "America gone mad with materialism . . . at a sexless and soulless America." Bitterly he asked: "How many hypocrites are there in America? How many trembling lambs, fearful of discovery? What authority have we set up over ourselves, that we are not as we are? What conspirators have power to determine our mode of consciousness, our sexual enjoyments, our different labors and loves?"[13]

Jack Kerouac's novels, most notably *On the Road* and *Dharma Bums,* portray characters who are tormented by their inability to realize true individualism. Kerouac's novels view the conventional workplace, religion, marriage, and recreation as being superficial and meaningless in their present forms. They prevent people from discovering a deeper purpose in life. In a quasi-religious search for a more spiritual existence, Kerouac's characters most often find a higher truth when they act on the impulses prescribed by their inner natures. The beat writers, together with the cult that sprang up around them, however, were more than mere literary figures. The stereotypical beatnik world of beards, sandals, coffee houses, convoluted poetry, unstructured music, hallucinogenic drugs, and Eastern religions was widely known because of popular magazines and, most important, because of a new form of communication known as television.[14]

Hallucinogenic drugs and Eastern religions were especially important to the hard-core member of the beat generation. They were vehicles used to purge oneself of the false beliefs of the existing order and to help one find a more meaningful existence. Psychedelic drugs were made popular in the United States by psychologist Timothy Leary. Inspired by Aldous Huxley's experiences with mescaline, Leary experimented with similar drugs during his tenure as a professor of psychology at Harvard University. Leary, a charismatic and flamboyant character, preached that people needed to "drop out" of conventional society in order to become "tuned in" to a higher truth. According to Leary, conventional society, or the "overground," as he called it, "is always obsessively and specifically organized. . . . Today the whole social structure is listed alphabetically in the yellow pages of the phone book." On the other hand, those who became "tuned in" to the underground could expect to experience a world in which "knowledge is experiential, whispered word of mouth, friend to friend and rarely written down. . . . The telephone directory has no listing for the soft essences, the chemical secretions of life . . . that warm hand that slips under your pretenses and touches you in exactly the right place." It is easy to see that Leary was disillusioned for the very same reasons as were the more respectable members of the intelligentsia, and his quest, although less conventional, was directed at recapturing the very same principles.[15]

The antimaterialism doctrines of Eastern religions, most notably Zen Buddhism, were also important in the beatnik's quest to find a more meaningful order in which to live. Eastern religions taught that the temporal trappings of life, when viewed in terms of a constantly changing and incomprehensible universe, were merely temporary illusions with no real lasting value. Eastern doctrines viewed reason as being meaningless because higher truths can only be experienced through an intuitive linking with the cosmos.

In the 1960s disillusionment was manifested in the counterrevolution. Groups such as the Student Nonviolent Coordination Committee (SNCC) and Students for a Democratic Society (SDS) were loosely organized, ad hoc committees that were centered on American college campuses. They used marches, sit-ins, and public political statements to hammer away at "the establishment," a buzz phrase for the conventional order, which they thought had suppressed individualism and opportunity in America. Along with a host of local issues, the movement mainly focused on civil rights and the military-industrial complex and its perceived role in promoting the Vietnam War.

In spite of its radical reputation, the counterrevolution was inextricably tied to the same traditional, naive myths that had been affecting American thinking since the nation's inception. These myths are clearly reflected in "The Port Huron Statement," a statement of principle issued in 1962 by a number of highly visible leaders of the movement. The "radical" document, as it was perceived to be at the time, argued that people must have "real choices and the resources to make those choices, or democracy is a fraud." With revolutionary defiance, the so-called radical leaders of the counterrevolution pronounced that

> we regard men [apparently women were excluded] as infinitely precious and possessed with unfulfilled capacities for reason, freedom and love. . . . We oppose the depersonalization that reduces human beings to the status of things. . . . We see little reason why men cannot meet with increasing skill the complexities and responsibilities of their situation, if society is organized not for minority, but for majority participation in decision making.

. . . The goal of man and society should be human independence: a concern not with image of popularity but with finding a meaning in life that is personally authentic.[16]

The declarations contained in this document make it clear that these so-called radicals were responding to the perceived loss of the same principles that theologians, educators, and health evangelists had sought to restore during the first two cycles of myth restoration. The criticisms of the counterrevolution differed little from those of the more conventional critics. Both elements believed that power needed to be decentralized and returned to the people. They, like all Americans, were acculturated to believe that people are rational and have the capacity to determine what is best for themselves as well as for the nation as a whole.

Some members of the counterrevolution used drugs and Eastern religions in much the same manner as the beatniks of the 1950s. In the 1960s hallucinogenic drugs were joined in popularity by a wide range of "uppers," "downers," and the ever-popular recreational drug, marijuana. In matters of religion, the Krishna movement replaced Zen Buddhism in popularity, but both contained the same therapeutic message for those searching for greater personal authenticity. The Krishnas joyfully prophesied that the materialistic age of Kali-Uga was about to end and that it would be replaced with an age in which the world would be united in peace and harmony. A smaller sect known as the Healthy-Happy-Holy Organization (3HO), however, introduced the nation to one of the most popular cultural symbols of the time. It pronounced that the world was in a significant period of transition between the two-thousand-year-long materialistic Piscean Age and the more spiritual Aquarian Age. Followers predicted that the Age of Aquarius would be fully established by the early years of the twenty-first century and, at that time, there would exist a unified global culture more in harmony with God.[17]

The beatnik scene and the antics of the counterrevolution alienated the average American in the 1950s and 1960s because they, as yet, were not disillusioned to the same degree as the fringe elements. By the early 1970s, however, they too were beginning to show signs of disillusionment. In 1978 sociologists Albert Bergensen and Mark Warr completed a study that revealed that the traditional seats of authority (the establishment), such as the federal government, the Supreme Court, organized religion, education, medicine, and the scientific community, were all viewed with increased skepticism.[18] The University of Michigan Election Studies Center conducted polls in the late 1950s and early 1960s and then again in the 1970s that indicated the very same trend. In the earlier polls, 69 percent of Americans agreed that "the people running the government in Washington are smart people who know what they are doing." By the 1970s, that figure had been reduced to just 29 percent. In the early 1960s, only 28 percent agreed that the government was run for the "benefit of a few big interests," but by the late 1970s, this figure had mushroomed to 65 percent.[19]

Such trends were also reflected in the Louis Harris polls that were conducted in the 1960s and then again in the 1980s. The percentage of those who agreed with the statement that the government had no interest in the opinions of the average citizen and that, in fact, federal bureaucrats were prone to take advantage of them rose during this period from a meager one-third minority to a two-thirds majority. Equally disturbing, the *Connecticut Mutual Life Report* on values in the 1980s concluded that "half of Americans (51 percent) do not believe that important national problems, such as energy shortages, inflation and crime can be solved through traditional American politics."[20]

EXPERIMENTATION AND MYTH RESTORATION

Historians have traditionally depicted each of the past three decades as having unique and distinctive qualities. Although this perspective certainly has merit, it could also be argued that one could profit from viewing the entire period as one chapter in

American history because Americans in the three decades shared similar concerns based on the frustration that resulted from believing in the same naive myths. Most important, the three decades were similar because Americans looked to similar therapeutic devices to find the elusive America described in myth.

In the mid-twentieth century, Americans again became conscious of the gap between the rich and the poor and the unacceptable levels of debilitating behavior. For a third time in American history, educational reform was seen as a key element in creating a true democracy in America with real opportunities for all of its citizens and in creating the kind of citizen who could actually possess freedom and still act responsibly. Ironically, beginning in the early 1950s, severe criticism was leveled at the very educational programs that were designed earlier in the century to accomplish these goals. Relativism, so important to the educational doctrines of Dewey, was assailed in the 1950s for its permissiveness and laxity in moral training and for its low academic standards. A former Connecticut school teacher, Mortimer Smith, in *And Madly Teach,* charged that "here was a doctrine that released the teacher from his responsibility for handing on the traditional knowledge of the race, a doctrine that firmly implied that one need not adhere to any standards of doctrine." Whereas Dewey called for the replacement of rote learning with a more vocational, hands-on learning experience, critics were now pointing to an overemphasis on vocational training as a major cause of the lack of standards in American education. Smith concluded that apparently "hairdressing and embalming are just as important, if not a little more so, than history and philosophy."[21]

The creation and management of educational systems and the bureaucracies that this created were also offensive to the critics of progressive forms of education. Education expert Diane Ravitch concluded that these early criticisms of progressive education were based on a fear of centralized authority. According to

Ravitch, it "enlarged the power of the social group and the state at the expense of the individual and his family." Consequently, she concluded that experts, such as Smith, were concerned that the emphasis on "adjusting the individual to society" had effectively "eroded individual freedom and fed the tendency in modern society to bureaucratic control by experts accountable to no one."[22]

These concerns, combined with the Russian launch of Sputnik in 1957, had an enormous effect on the course that education would take thereafter. The display of Russian technological superiority was considered additional evidence that education in America was inferior. The Sputnik affair, combined with a new sensitivity in the 1960s to inequality and widespread poverty, resulted in the federal government's allocating funds for education in unprecedented amounts. Educators, under the illusion that all can learn equally well, experimented with new classroom environments and with new methods of teaching the three R's. Also, reformers innocently assumed that greater numbers of people receiving better educations would translate into more economic success for the individual, thus narrowing the gap between the rich and the poor.

Today, disillusionment with low educational standards is still widespread. The media have devoted much attention to the why-Johnny-can't-read issue as well as to the soaring dropout rate. In 1983 the government-appointed National Commission on Excellence in Education announced that American students did not measure up to those in other industrialized nations. The Commission's report, "A Nation at Risk," found that twenty-three million American adults and 13 percent of all seventeen-year-olds are functionally illiterate. Even more alarming, it reported that the "average achievement of high school students on most standardized tests is now lower than 26 years ago when Sputnik was launched." To make matters worse, the decline in intellectual achievement in America, according to the report, had come at a time when high technology was transforming "every aspect of our lives."[23]

The National Commission on Excellence in Education concluded that the solution to America's educational woes lay in returning to the "basics," or more accurately the "new basics." The new basics consists of the old basics — English, mathematics, science, and social studies — plus computer science. The return to the basics in education is necessary because, according to the Commission, "Secondary school curricula have been homogenized, diluted, and diffused to the point that they no longer have a central purpose." Much like Mortimer Smith's satirical comments in 1949 about the overemphasis on hairdressing and embalming in school curricula, the 1983 report stated that "in effect, we have cafeteria-style curriculum in which appetizers and desserts can easily be mistaken for the main course."[24]

Four years after "A Nation at Risk" appeared, Secretary of Education William Bennett personally penned what in retrospect appears to be two politically self-serving reports on the state of education in America. In "James Madison High School" (1987) and "James Madison Elementary School" (1988), Mr. Bennett announced, with enough precaution to cover himself, that the war against ignorance in America was well on its way to be being won. He based his conclusions on the number of school districts that were rushing to adopt the and "back to the basics," or the "essentialist," view of education. Self-serving political rhetoric aside, it remains to be seen whether this round of educational experimentation will have a lasting impact on improving education in America. However, for some, the essentialist movement will serve as a myth restoration vehicle because it will convince them that individuals will be able to compete more effectively and that the gap between the rich and poor will close; America will then realize its image as the land of opportunity.[25]

Public awareness, another form of education, continues to play an important role in myth restoration, and the important role of television in generating public awareness cannot be overstressed. Television, like the lyceum and the Chautauqua movements, serves to inform and misinform the public on issues of national concern. Television is at once a molder and a reflector of American opinion and, unwittingly in that role, serves as a cohesive factor in American culture. Situation comedies and dramas subtly allow Americans to live vicariously the kind of life prescribed in myth. Furthermore, television programs, especially talk shows, provide a showcase for the most recent trends in theological, educational, and physiological therapies — therapies that offer a measure of hope to viewers. These talk shows, if nothing else, serve as a forum for catharsis in which viewers can find comfort in learning that they are not alone in their imperfect existence. Unfortunately, television, like the lyceum and Chautauqua movements, has provided a stage for hucksters peddling get-rich-quick schemes and all manner of health panaceas to an audience made vulnerable by the innocence of its cultural myths.

Few would disagree that the nation is currently undergoing yet another prohibition movement. Media buzz phrases, such as "the war on crime" and "the war on drugs," have made alcohol and drug abuse the number one issue of concern in America today. Even under these negative conditions, public awareness serves an important role in myth restoration. These issues, now so paramount in the thinking of Americans, serve as scapegoats for many other problems in the nation. The media and their ability to heighten public awareness are also contributing to the belief that failure in America is not a systemic matter but rather the fault of a few Colombian drug lords.

The media have also been instrumental in focusing the public eye on pornography and its relationship to sexually related crimes. The so-called sexual revolution of the 1960s and its ramifications have now led to a backlash in many sectors of the society. Most disturbing, pornography has even caught the attention of the federal government, as evidenced by the expenditure of $500,000 in 1988 for a year-long, two-volume, 190-page report on the subject.

According to public opinion analyst Daniel Yankelovich, Americans today suffer from an "odd feeling of estrangement from the world." They have become preoccupied of late with questions such as "How can I find self-fulfillment? . . . How can I GROW? How can I best realize the commitment I have to develop myself." According to Yankelovich, they "do not see themselves as part and parcel of an ongoing world, progressively discovering themselves in relation to their work, their friends, families and the much larger society. Rather they are isolated — some might say existential — units, related intimately only to their own psyches." Beginning in the 1970s, some of these Americans became involved in one or more human potential therapies. Many others are actively pursuing any number of diet and exercise regimens.[26]

Like theology and education, the appeal of human potential therapies rests on the promise to make individuals more competitive in the race to achieve material success and in the quest to find spiritual and aesthetic fulfillment. Human potential therapies fall into three categories. The first category derives its therapeutic value from its promise to allow individuals to once again take charge of their lives. Erhard Sensitivity Training (est), for example, indoctrinates its followers to believe that nothing can happen to an individual that is not willed by that individual.[27]

Peter Marin's account of a conversation with an est graduate indicates how absurd this philosophy can become when carried to the extreme. A female graduate of est indicated that she felt sorry for the hungry and poor but that they "must have wished it on themselves," and that a friend of hers who had been raped and murdered "was to be pitied for having willed it to occur."[28] Ironically, the problem-solving assumption of est is closely related to the problem-solving assumption of conservative Christianity. While fundamentalist Christianity teaches that humans have free will and are therefore solely responsible for their sins, *est* teaches that humans have free will and are therefore solely responsible for their failures.

The second category of human potential therapies promises to teach individuals to rise above earthly imperfection. Transpersonal psychology and transcendental meditation promise to help people find exactness and certainty, and with it greater peace and prosperity, through transcendence. The *Journal of Transpersonal Psychology* described this form of human potential movement as providing "ultimate values, unitive consciousness, peak experience, being, essence, bliss, awe, wonder, self-actualization, ultimate states, transcendence, spirit, sacralization of everyday life, oneness, cosmic awareness, cosmic play." Psychologist Abraham Maslow, one of the guiding lights in the human potential movement, defined transcendence as "getting off the merry-go-round. Walking through the abattoir without getting bloody. To be clean even in the midst of filth." Thus, in a manner similar to the born-again Christian, the individual is able to view earthly imperfection "as if one were looking upon it objectively, detachedly from a great and impersonal or superpersonal height."[29]

Although most Americans are not involved in the aforementioned categories of human potential therapies, there are a significant number of them who pursue the same elusive goals through the aid of self-help books. Books such as *Looking Out for Number One, Self Creation, Pulling Your Own Strings, How to Be Your Own Best Friend, Your Erroneous Zones, How I Found Freedom in an Unfree World,* and *When All You've Ever Wanted Isn't Enough* are but a few of the many that carry the same fundamental message as the more extreme therapies mentioned previously.[30]

More recently, physiological redemption, the third human potential category, has enjoyed enormous popularity. Although extreme doctrines such as autogenics, autofeedback, and psychokinesis must be included in this category, the vast majority of Americans are involved in less spectacular forms of physical redemption. Millions of Americans have participated in or are presently engaged in one or more health, diet, or exercise regimens. Health consciousness is another of the media themes that has become all-consuming in American thinking. As early as 1981, Americans spent $5 billion on health foods and vitamins and $50 million on diet and exercise books. In addition, health club and fitness club membership fees for that year totaled an unprecedented $5 billion. In 1985 four of the top ten best-selling books dealt with diet and exercise. In 1987 Americans spent an estimated $74 billion on low-calorie foods and over $2 billion on vitamins. Sales of name-brand athletic shoes reached the $6 billion mark in 1987, triple the amount spent in 1977. Even more dramatic, sales of home exercise equipment skyrocketed from a mere $5 million in 1977 to $738 million in 1987.[31]

Time magazine indicated that wellness is a quasi religion in America. Jack Lalane, whose name has long been synonymous with physical fitness, wrote that "when you quit exercising, you let go. The devil will get you." A recent issue of *Time* observed that "if today's temple of the body is the health spa, its altar is the Nautilus machine and its Bible is *Prevention* [the health magazine]." The editors of *American Health* wrote:

> The formula used to be simple — work hard, get married, have kids, buy a home . . . and be happy. It was the American Dream and it was enough. Not anymore. The safe world of Ozzie and Harriet and Father Knows Best has been replaced by the complexity of Thirty Something. We're trying to have it all — not just a nice home and family but a challenging job, exciting hobbies and new chances for self expression. Call it the new American dream. To be a super achiever you need stamina; you need a strong body as well as a strong mind.[32]

And yet, as Barry Glassner wrote, "All our efforts to beautify and condition our bodies have not made us, as a nation, any happier with the way we look." Physician-philosopher Lewis Thomas similarly notes that "we Americans have become a nation of healthy hypochondriacs, living gingerly, worrying ourselves to death."[33] If abundance had not erased a reverence for the past in American culture, the pronouncements of *Time* and *American Health* would not seem so startling. They are, in fact, quite reminiscent of the preachings of Sylvester Graham in the early nineteenth century and of the likes of Bernarr MacFadden in the early twentieth century.

Unfortunately, nativism continues to be an important outlet for some Americans in their quest to realize the kind of life represented in mythology. These individuals have found new, and in some cases familiar, scapegoats to serve as antidotes for their anxieties. During the first period of cultural distortion, Mormons, Masons, and Catholics were the objects of such paranoia. During the second period of cultural distortion, there were the heretics espousing Darwinian scientific principles, domestic radicals ranging from labor leaders to communists, and a hodgepodge of "unfit" southern European immigrants.

Part of the recent nativistic impulse has been directed at Latin American immigrants. Congress has established immigration laws similar to those in the early twentieth century in order to prevent migrating Hispanics from threatening the American dream. There is also an increasing number of reports of racially motivated violence occurring between blacks and whites, both in the North and in the South. Racist organizations such as the Order, Aryan Nations, the Ku Klux Klan, and the Covenant, the Sword, and the Arm of the Lord are experiencing increased enrollments once again.

It could be argued that bureaucrats, the "experts" who were looked to with such hope as the nation's saviors early in the twentieth century, have now become the ultimate target of nativistic impulses. This form of disillusionment began with Howard Jarvis and the middle-class taxpayer's revolt in the 1970s and continued to be reflected in the current conservative political mood of the nation. No clearer statement of the disillusionment with scientific management can be found than in the

symbolic role that Ronald Reagan has played in American politics in the past decade. Reagan's popularity, like that of the *Dirty
Harry* and *Rambo* movies, rests on the renewed glorification of
self-reliance in seeking justice and on the promotion of greater
economic opportunity for the individual. The dispassionate and
indifferent bureaucrat, so praised in the early twentieth century,
has now become the obstacle to justice in the Clint Eastwood and
Sylvester Stallone classics and appears to the average American
as an obstacle in daily life. Thus, it is only fitting that Reagan, the
"Dirty Harry" of politics, has become the symbol of a new
threatened and disadvantaged element in American society —
the middle-class silent majority. The fact that today the federal
bureaucracy is larger and more complex than ever is totally
insignificant in the nation's perception of Reagan. He continues
to personify the notion that America is a land of opportunity
where there is enough for all and a place where those who strive
for success will have it *if,* and only *if,* they are unobstructed by
oppressive authority.[34]

Traditionally, twentieth-century analysts have viewed recent cynicism in America in terms of the political, social, and
economic problems of the recent past — such as the Vietnam
War, the 1972 Watergate break-in and the subsequent revelations
of wrongdoing in the highest echelons of the federal government, and the energy crisis prompted by the OPEC oil embargo
in 1973. Although there is no doubt that these events did contribute to disillusionment, it could be argued that they merely
reinforced the disillusionment and anxiety that has been brew-
ing since the scientifically managed state came into existence
in the 1930s. In the 1950s one could already see the early signs
of disillusionment in the continuing criticism of progressive
education; in concerns about excessive materialism and conformity consciousness expressed by Riesman, Whyte, and others; in the search for personal authenticity undertaken by the
beat writers; and, of course, in the myriad protests undertaken

by the counterculture in the 1960s. Clearly the depth and breadth of disillusionment during this period cannot be linked to any one event or series of events. It has its roots in the perceived threats to the continuation of the naive myths born out of abundance and sustained by abundance.

5.
The Golden Age of High Technology?

I have argued that Edenic expectations of land frontiers, machine technology, and scientific management played an important role in allowing Americans to continue to cling to naive key national myths. Today, high technology may be on the verge of playing the same role. Although the average American is not yet caught up in the excitement created by visions of an approaching golden age of high technology, futurist writers certainly are. There is no shortage of books and articles that tell of the important role that high-tech communications, robotics, genetic engineering, and space colonization will play in the building of a bountiful, equitable, and more fulfilling world in which to live. Tragically, futurist writings unintentionally affirm many of the same naive assumptions about America that were discussed in the previous chapters.

Enthusiasts of high-tech communications have written that, among their many benefits, these technologies will contribute to the wider distribution of education, the dismantling of government bureaucracies, and the decentralization of the economy. Arthur C. Clarke, of *2001: A Space Odyssey* fame, has predicted that the hand-held electronic pocket tutor will revolutionize education worldwide because it will make formal school settings and teachers obsolete. The pocket tutor will become so cheap that everyone will be able to afford one. "The electronic tutor," Clarke wrote, "will spread across the planet as swiftly as the transistor radio, with even more momentous consequences." From the rain forests of Borneo to the mountains of West Virginia, an education will be available to almost every citizen on the face of the earth. Clarke anticipates that as many people become educated, the distribution of resources will become more equitable throughout the world. Also it is assumed that a more educated society is a more harmonious society because of a more enlightened citizenry.[1]

The eminent psychologist Carl Rogers is another who has eagerly looked to high-tech communications to produce a more "person-centered mode of education," which will magnify the desire to learn and thus lead to a wider range of people gaining confidence in themselves. Students would be encouraged, Rogers wrote, "to prize themselves, to develop self-confidence and self-esteem." The end result would be a community of global dimensions "in which the destructive competition of today would be replaced by cooperation, respect for others, and mutual helpfulness."[2]

James Martin is one of the high-tech communications enthusiasts who sees developments in this field acting as a deterrent to encroaching federal bureaucracies. He insists that bureaucracies inadvertently hoard information, and in doing so, they frustrate the evolution of democratic institutions. Most data, although public, is rarely accessed. Once the public is able to access this information through viewdata systems (two-way communication systems using television monitors and telephone hookups), numerous benefits will result because Martin assumes that rational, public-minded citizens will use such information wisely to benefit themselves as well as society as a whole. "Who knows," Martin wrote, "a little old lady in the Bronx may learn how to use econometric models via her home TV terminal and may make suggestions about how to improve the government's economic policy."[3]

An additional concern of those applauding the benefits of high-tech communications is the overly centralized economy in America and especially its effect on community cohesiveness. According to Loy Singleton, decentralization will take place in virtually all sectors of the economy, including the production of energy. The portrait that Singleton paints of the future is wonderfully bucolic. He portrays a land of happy, contented citizens busily earning their daily bread in the comfort of their own homes. In this idyllic setting, one pictures citizens occasionally pausing during their work on their computer terminals to gaze out the window at a peaceful countryside of rolling hills and small villages. This high-tech "middle landscape" of the future is interrupted only by the occasional windmill blissfully churning out electricity and with it a symbolic vision of the kind of society portrayed in the nation's paradisiacal self-image.[4]

Unfortunately, the predictions of James Martin, Loy Singleton, Arthur C. Clarke, and Carl Rogers are an indication that American culture continues to cling to the same old tired myths that have plagued America since its inception. These writers assume that there is a direct link between the distribution of education and the distribution of an altered and more idyllic form of human behavior. They also assume that the distribution of material goods is linked to altruism and voluntary responsible behavior. Their vision differs little from that of Timothy Walker, who in 1832 predicted that as a result of the machine "there would be nothing to hinder all mankind from becoming philosophers, poets, and votaries of art" and "the whole time and thought of the human race could be given to inward culture and spiritual improvement." The global harmony theme of the high-tech communications enthusiasts is not new. One is reminded of Samuel Morse's assessment of the importance of the Atlantic cable completed in 1858. He predicted when the cable was completed that "an instrument has been established to end the isolation of the nations of the world, and surely an era of peace awaits the world."[5]

Robotics is also a part of the scenario of the golden age that awaits the world in the future. Currently, robots are used mostly for assembling, welding, and painting in manufacturing processes. The robots that have futurists so excited are the so-called smart robots. These units will be capable of performing tasks that require situational judgments, and thus they will have the capability to perform a much wider range of more complex tasks. It could be argued that robots will displace workers and that this will lead to severe economic disruption. Marvin Cetron and Thomas O'Toole are two futurists who anticipate this concern by arguing that robotics will create so many new economic opportunities that the economic disruption will be minimal and temporary; in fact, productivity will increase to such an extent that prosperity will be experienced by a larger number of people than ever before.[6]

I am not arguing here that technology in and of itself is dangerous but rather that it is the mind-set that makes use of it that can be dangerous. For example, Cetron and O'Toole argue that women will be the "biggest winners in the rush to robotize the nation's factories." Yet, when they describe these factories of the future, they display an incredible insensitivity to women and the economic inequality that women still face in the marketplace today. The future industrial workplace will make "brawn, strength and the ability to tolerate noise and dirt on the job" unnecessary. The factories of the future will require the kind of people "who can sit down at keyboards all day long, shift after shift, and punch out the programs that start the robots, keep them going, change their direction when they have to and tell them when to stop." Where will the skills for this type of labor come from? They will come from the "stenographer's" pool. From this revelation one can assume that the majority of managerial positions in the golden age of high technology will still largely be held by males.[7]

Theologians, educators, and physiological therapists of the past and present have all struggled to try to make people conform to the naive image portrayed in national myth. With the development of genetic engineering, humanity will have yet another opportunity to fantasize about achieving this elusive goal. Since scientists have broken the DNA code, the genetic blueprint of human life-forms, scientific and medical journals have been littered with articles about the exciting prospects of this development.

Perhaps the most intriguing, and at the same time the most frightening, aspect of genetic engineering is the potential that exists for parents to design their children. G. Harry Stine wrote that "children produced by genetic mappings and selection will eventually be superior to randomly conceived children in terms of congenital defects and other undesirable inherited traits." Stine insists, however, that the procedure will be a matter of personal choice, but then he threatens readers with the prospect that "if you don't participate, your children won't be able to compete in the world."[8]

Haunting visions of social Darwinism appear when Stine assesses the role of children who are born without the benefit of genetic mapping. These children, he says, will "become the 'controls,' the basic unselected strain to which the genetically selected children are always compared to insure that selection has not been progressing along undesirable lines." The prospect of genetic engineering raises an important question. Who will determine what is desirable and what is undesirable in human behavior? Stine's answer to this question contains the predictable antibureaucracy sentiment that is so prevalent in the nation today. Centralized authority, he insists (Orwellian visions come to mind here), poses the greatest danger to the misuse of genetic engineering. To avoid this threat, decisions on matters pertaining to genetic engineering must be placed in the hands of the scientific equivalent of the local school board. Laws governing the design of human beings, in other words, are to be considered a matter of local option, much like liquor and obscenity laws. Apparently, Mr. Stine is willing to substitute the tyranny of the masses for oligarchic tyranny.[9]

To no one's surprise, Timothy Leary has joined the ranks of genetic engineering enthusiasts. Leary, displaying the same unbounded enthusiasm that he had for psychedelic drugs earlier on, now appears to be looking to genetic engineers to restore individualism in America. "Here is the ultimate step in active, confident self-determination. . . . This heroic band of frontier adventurers should be glamorized, publicized, gossiped about, profiled like rock stars, pro athletes, and politicians. The thrilling dramatic feats they perform should receive front-page coverage." He concludes that "everytime they score a point, humanity evolves a notch. Rah. Rah. Rah."[10]

Upon reading Stine's and Leary's accounts of genetic engineering, one is reminded of the *American Polytechnic Journal*, which in 1853 declared that the inventor of the machine age "should be elevated on the highest pinnacle of greatness; his place is in the largest and richest temple yet erected in the country." The innocent confidence that these futurists have in genetic engineering is similar to that of the *American Journal of Science* when in 1840 it asked: "What is there yet to be done upon the face of the earth, that cannot be affected by the powers of the human mind. . . . Man . . . is, indeed, 'lord of creation.' "[11]

Finally, space colonization, because of the efforts of respected physicist Gerard K. O'Neill, is also emerging as one of the saviors of the future. O'Neill, more than anyone else, is responsible for removing space colonization from the realm of science fiction and placing it within the context of serious scientific inquiry. He has convinced the scientific community, as well as highly placed officials in the government, that space colonization is feasible within the present bounds of technology. Unfortunately, he also displays the same innocent view of human nature that has plagued this nation time and time again. Among other things, O'Neill has insisted that space technology can make "unlimited low-cost energy available to everyone rather than just to those nations favored with large reserves of fossil or nuclear fuels." He predicts that "stealing or killing or polluting" will stop because there will be "an unlimited materials source." Space colonization, according to O'Neill, will also increase "individual freedom and the range of options available to every human being." He unwittingly assumes that in the future it won't be just Americans who will have all that they want; rather, citizens all over the world will bask in this same luxury. O'Neill depicts space colonization as the culmination of the human quest for greater personal freedom but without the dreadful consequences that have accompanied it in the past.[12]

Like many other futurists, O'Neill holds a strong antibureaucracy bias. "I leave it as an exercise for the reader to list all the federal agencies that obviously would be unnecessary in a space colony," he wrote. According to O'Neill, food and energy will be in such abundance that there will be no need for government agencies to scrutinize the distribution of these commodities. Even more incredible, he suggests that space colonies will be "far enough from others not to require defense."[13]

Although there are numerous Edenic accounts of the future, their enthusiasm is not yet shared by the average American. If the past is any guide, one should expect an initial measure of skepticism. No doubt there will be those who will articulate the dangers posed by new developments. High-tech communications, robotics, genetic engineering, and space colonization may even be criticized by someone as eloquent as Sinclair Lewis, who bitterly attacked the impact of industrialization on rural life in the late nineteenth century. Lewis described rural America at that time as a place characterized by its "unimaginatively standardized background, a sluggishness of speech and manners, a rigid ruling of the spirit by the desire to appear respectable. . . . It is slavery self-sought and self-defended." In dreary tones of disillusionment, Lewis spoke of "a savorless people, gulping tasteless food, and sitting afterward, coatless and thoughtless, in rocking-chairs prickly with inane decorations, listening to mechanical music, saying mechanical things about the excellence of Ford automobiles, and viewing themselves as the greatest race in the world."[14]

It is difficult to predict whether this nation will continue its idyllic flights of fancy. It may be that as this nation returns to a more normal historical state (characterized by a historical pattern established over thousands of years rather than over just a few hundred years), it will develop a more realistic perception of itself. I suspect, however, that because the perception of abundance still lingers in American culture today, this nation's immaturity will persist for a while longer. No doubt in the twenty-first century we will be receiving letters from friends and relatives living in space colonies, and these letters will be similar in tone to those received from the Ohio frontier in the early nineteenth century. We will learn that life is "happy and healthy" in outer space and that there are no "sickly, hysterical wives" and "no dyspeptic men constantly swallowing the nostrums of quacks." We will be reminded, as were those in the late nineteenth century, of how wonderful it is to live in an age "which for its inventions and discoveries, its improvements in intelligence and virtue, stands without a rival in the history of the world."[15] When reading about such wondrous things, however, I fear that we will still be sitting in rocking chairs "prickly with inane decorations, listening to mechanical music, saying mechanical things" about automobiles, only this time Japanese automobiles, and still saying that we are "the greatest race [nation] in the world."

Epilogue ❧

What lies ahead for America if it approaches the future with the same naivete that it has demonstrated in the past? The answer to this question is quite disturbing. Most alarming, a combination of decreased economic opportunities and a continued rise in population could lead to serious economic problems that could spark levels of social and political turmoil never witnessed before in this nation.

Between 1950 and 1986, America's population rose by approximately seventy-seven million despite a decline in the birth rate. Most of the increase occurred between 1950 and 1965 as a result of the post–World War II baby boom and a recent rise in immigration. Certainly there have been dramatic increases in American population in the past. However, in former times the pressures of population growth were matched by national economic growth. Thus, even though the average American received a disproportional share of the economic pie, overall growth of the pie resulted in an increase in the size of the disproportional share. Today, unlike in the past, because of a slower rate of economic growth it may no longer be possible for increased economic productivity to disguise inequity. There are increasing signs that this disparity is occurring already. For example, between 1968 and 1981 real wages for the average American declined by 20 percent.

Economic historians indicate that this decline is due, in part, to the decline in the nation's rate of industrial productivity. The average annual increase in industrial productivity between 1948 and 1966 was 3.4 percent. During the next seven years, the increase in productivity slowed to 2.3 percent. Between 1973 and

1977, the rate of increase slumped to just 1 percent before dropping to 0.4 percent the following year. Beginning in 1979, productivity failed to increase at all and in fact began to decline.[1]

Similar trends characterize the nation's relative position in the world economy. In 1947, for example, America produced 60 percent of the world's industrial goods. By 1979 that figure had dropped to just 35 percent. Furthermore, since 1963 American exports of manufactured goods have reflected a downward trend. Between 1963 and 1981, America's share of the automobile market fell by 33 percent. During the same period, sales of agricultural machinery declined by 40 percent, just as sales in telecommunication equipment fell by 50 percent.[2]

The implications here are very serious because as economic mobility decreases, class lines will become more clearly defined and more enduring from generation to generation. As this occurs it will become more and more difficult to explain failure merely in terms of poor national leadership or in terms of individual failure. People may be consciously and unwittingly forced to look more closely at the system that governs their daily lives. In other words, ideology will for the first time play an important role in American politics. For better or for worse, the present American political scene is characterized by two main clusters of interest groups formally organized into the Democratic and Republican political parties. Both parties, although rivals on the political scene, share the same assumptions about the function of society, and both parties are driven by the same set of myths that has produced such tragic consequences in the past. Members of both parties hold their offices by appealing to the majority interest, not to what the founding fathers termed the whole interest. Citizens themselves contribute to this practice because they have been acculturated to see the whole in terms of their own specific needs.

If, as suggested, class lines become more recognizable, the average American may look more seriously at other ideological options. Some of these options may challenge the basic premises upon which the two present ruling clusters of interest groups operate, and thus it could be argued that it will be more difficult to effect a peaceful transferal of power.

What issues will lead to the promotion of increased class conflict and greater ideological struggle in American politics? Most Americans are aware of, although indifferent to, dangerous international trends that threaten all people living on this planet. The depletion of the rain forests, the thinning of the ozone layer, global warming, and the continued threat posed by overpopulation and mass starvation are just a few of the problems that will reach critical proportions in the near future. And the media have made most Americans aware of crime and drug problems of epidemic proportions.

Although these developments are extremely important to national and international survival, there are other trends, more local in focus, that are equally disturbing and, in my judgment, pose a more immediate threat to the cultural stability of the United States. It is evident that as our society strains with more limited resources to care for its members, it will become increasingly difficult to reconcile the contradictions that exist between America's self-image as a land of opportunity and the reality that its citizens face on a daily basis. In my judgment, these inconsistencies will be exposed first at both ends of the age spectrum, among the aged and among infants.

There is no question that America's population is getting older. In the early nineteenth century, over 50 percent of Americans were children under the age of sixteen. By the mid-1980s, that number had been reduced to only 22 percent. Presently, less than 38 percent of American families have children under the age of 18. According to Alan Pifer and Lydia Bronte, consultants with the Carnegie Corporation, an ever-increasing proportion of children born in our society are black or Hispanic, and they will receive a disproportionately small share of the nation's resources. "Hidden away in deteriorating inner-city areas out of the sight of the average middle-class voter," Pifer and Bronte warn, "these minority children may seem to be of little importance to the larger society." Pifer and Bronte conclude that "in a situation where so few adults feel any direct personal stake in the quality, or even the availability of essential services for children, it is all too easy for those services to atrophy and decline."[3] Once neglect of children in America reaches scandalous proportions and the initial process of casting about for a scapegoat is completed, the system is all that will remain to be scrutinized.

Looking at the other end of the age spectrum, improved medical technology is creating a longer life span for the average citizen. The number of Americans aged sixty-five and older has more than doubled since 1950, and the number of citizens aged eighty-five and older has more than quadrupled since that time. By the year 2000, over 20 percent of the American population will consist of citizens that we currently consider to be past retirement age. The implications of this simple demographic fact are enormous. Given the current retirement age of sixty-five, or in some cases seventy, our nation will be faced with a large proportion of its retired population still having a considerable number of years to live. Thus, upcoming generations will be much less patient with the present practice of warehousing elderly citizens in institutions until death removes them as a burden to society. Senior citizens are already demanding that they be allowed to live out their lives in an active and dignified manner.[4]

An integral part of senior citizens' expectations is the benefits they will receive from the social security system that they have helped support all of their working lives. Unfortunately, the social security system is already overburdened and will be strained to its limits given the current trends in aging. Sociologist Paul Zopf, Jr., reports that the social security payroll tax has increased "from 5.2 percent on maximum taxable earnings of $7,800 in 1971, to 6.7 percent on a maximum of $32,700 in 1982, to an already legislated 7.65 percent on a maximum of $66,900 in 1990, and wage earners face even greater increases after that in order to support the aging baby-boom population."[5]

Furthermore, if one introduces the high cost of Medicare and other federally sponsored programs into the equation, the consequences become frightening beyond comprehension. Currently, the elderly (12 percent of the population) consume 30 percent of the federal budget. By the year 2030, the elderly (20 percent of the population) will take up 60 percent of the federal budget. Malcolm Morrison, an expert on retirement and age discrimination, wrote that "it is difficult to foresee a social policy that would allocate three-fifths of the annual budget for support of the older population." This is especially true given the current federal deficit and the emphasis on budget cutting.[6]

The problems of an aging population have many tentacles that will have dire consequences. Some younger Americans are already growing resentful because they believe that the last generation created programs, such as the social security system, to ensure their own comfort past retirement age while passing the cost on to later generations. On the other hand, the elderly are becoming increasingly resentful of their inability to find a meaningful existence in a society that has largely put them in storage to await death.

Is there any reason to be optimistic about the future? In my opinion, the answer is no, and the historical pattern outlined in this text is chilling evidence for such a pessimistic conclusion. Abundance has provided Americans with such positive and immediate rewards for their actions that their assumptions about human nature have become overly optimistic and naive. As citizens of this nation gained more confidence in themselves, they abandoned most forms of higher authority, which they concluded were unnecessary infringements upon their personal liberty. Tragically, unparalleled abundance has insulated the average American from the realization that individual freedom has allowed them to inflict cruelties upon themselves and others.

We may want to heed the words of Herbert Croly, who in 1909 argued that "unfettered individualism" was responsible for the injustices in America at the turn of the century. Croly wisely realized that "practically unrestricted economic opportunities are precisely the condition which makes for bondage." Croly, of course, was referring to an economy that had become so distorted that 60 percent of the nation's wealth was controlled by just 2 percent of the population.[7]

The early twentieth century was also a time when some intellectual leaders, as well as clergymen and heads of business, counseled that support of the poor would only lead to the nation's ruination. This was a time when the nation was on the cutting edge of scientific sophistication and saw sterilization as an acceptable method of dealing with its unfit. Finally, this was a time when citizens of the land of opportunity established rigid immigration quotas to prevent undesirables from polluting the nation's white, Anglo-Saxon bloodlines. Beginning in the early nineteenth century and continuing to the present, Mormons, Masons, Irish Catholics, Italians, Poles, Orientals, blacks, and, most recently, Hispanics have all taken their turns as the recipients of discrimination and persecution.

Beginning in 1980, "unfettered individualism" and the wise free agent-citizen assaulted the unfit in more subtle ways. Americans and their leaders today see education, the environment, worker safety, health, housing, and nutrition as "social luxuries" that are too expensive to maintain. In 1953 with the creation of the Department of Health, Education and Welfare, it appeared as if Americans were beginning to recognize their social responsibilities. From 1950 to 1964, expenditures in this area of the budget rose from $35.1 billion to over $108 billion. Unfortunately, America's social consciousness eroded as the price tag of the Vietnam War increased at the end of the 1960s and throughout the 1970s. Of seven nations in 1977 — Canada, France, West Germany, Japan, Sweden, the United Kingdom, and the United States — only Japan allocated a smaller percentage of its gross national product to social welfare programs than did the United States.[8] Such erosion was accelerated in the 1980s as a result of President Reagan's deliberate effort to stimulate the economy from the top down and to trim dramatically the budget for social welfare programs.

When the failures and follies of America are considered in their totality, it is clear that its citizens have not used their freedom wisely. This should not be surprising given the ability of humans to rationalize and given that we have had unprecedented amounts of freedom to act upon our rationalizations. It is understandable that this nation has been able to do all manner of harm in the name of economic expediency and even in the name of God and intellectual enlightenment.

Can anything be done to prevent the troubling scenario outlined in this book from becoming reality? I have demonstrated that Americans have been engaged in the pursuit of a kind of society that has never existed and can never exist. Once again the culprit has been myths fostered and nourished by abundance or at least the perception of abundance. Two centuries of acculturation have prevented Americans from coming to grips with a simple reality: There are not enough resources for all to share equally if the standard of living is measured in terms of the middle and upper classes.

The fact is that if the white, Anglo-Saxon, middle-class majority of this nation wishes to continue to live at its present socioeconomic level, it must cut off the lower class and all others who, from its perspective, drain the economy. In other words, if the top 20 percent wishes to continue to control 40 percent of the nation's before-tax income as it has done since World War II, then it must eliminate even its current limited and patronizing gestures to the bottom 20 percent of society.[9] On the other hand, if we are sincere in our commitment to create a fair and equitable society, then we must recognize that all of us will have to live with less.

Notes ⚜

CHAPTER 1

1. Both society and culture are defined here simply as accumulations of assumptions, myths, and responses. When these are manifested in formal institutional arrangements, the term society is used, and when they are manifested in informal and voluntary behavior based on deep-seated assumptions, the term culture more aptly applies.

2. For further insights into this aspect of American culture, see Alexis de Tocqueville, *Democracy in America,* ed. Phillip Bradley (New York: Alfred A. Knopf, 1945); Thorsten Veblen, *The Theory of the Leisure Class* (New York: Charles Scribner's Sons, 1904); Mary Douglas and Baron Isherwood, *The World of Goods* (New York: Basic Books, 1979); and the essays in Richard W. Fox and T. Jackson Lears, eds., *The Culture of Consumption: Critical Essays in American History, 1880–1980* (New York: Pantheon Books, 1983).

3. See Frederick Merk, *Manifest Destiny and Mission in American History: A Reinterpretation* (New York: Vintage, 1963). For an interesting discussion of myth and its role in the creation of America's postwar ethos, see Michael Vlahos, "America's Postwar Ethos," *Foreign Affairs,* 66, no. 5 (Summer 1988): 1091. See also Sacvan Bercovitch, *The American Jeremiad* (Madison, Wis.: University of Wisconsin Press, 1978).

4. Stuart Bruchey, *The Wealth of the Nation: An Economic History of the United States* (New York: Harper & Row, 1988), 24.

5. Ibid., 24, 71.

6. Ibid., 67.

7. John A. Garraty, *The New Commonwealth, 1877–1890* (New York: Harper & Row, 1968), 80.

8. Ibid., 81.

9. Peter Laslett, *The World We Have Lost* (London: Methuen, 1965), 40–54; and Wallace Notestein, *The English People on the Eve of Colonization, 1603–1642* (New York: Harper, 1954), 70–85. See also Edward Pessen, *Riches, Class and Power Before the Civil War* (Lexington, Mass.: D. C. Heath, 1974), 31–43. The most comprehensive study of early nineteenth-century economic growth in the United States is still Stuart Bruchey, *The Roots of American Economic*

Growth, 1607–1861: An Essay in Social Causation (New York: Harper & Row, 1965).

10. Howard N. Ross, "Economic Growth and Change in the United States Under Laissez Faire: 1870–1929," in Frederic Cople Jaher, ed., *The Age of Industrialism in America: Essays in Social Structure and Cultural Values* (New York: Free Press, 1968), 6–42. See also John Chambers, *The Tyranny of Change: America in the Progressive Era, 1900–1917* (New York: St. Martin's Press, 1980), 73–104. Post–World War II statistics taken from U.S. Bureau of the Census, "Money Income in 1974 of Families and Persons in the United States," *Current Population Reports,* series P-60, no. 101, table 22, p. 37. See also Harrell R. Rodgers, Jr., *Poverty Amid Plenty: A Political and Economic Analysis* (Reading, Mass.: Addison-Wesley Co., 1979), 17–40.

11. Tocqueville, *Democracy in America,* 11.

12. Turner, Frederick Jackson, "The Significance of the Frontier in American History," in *American Historical Association Annual Report for the Year 1893,* 227. For a comprehensive discussion of the Turner thesis and its supporters and detractors, see Ray Allen Billington, *America's Frontier Heritage* (New York: Holt, Rinehart and Winston, 1966).

13. Walter Prescott Webb, *The Great Frontier* (Austin, Tex.: University of Texas Press, 1964).

14. David Potter, *People of Plenty* (Chicago: University of Chicago Press, 1954).

15. Especially relevant is Anthony F. C. Wallace, "Revitalization Movements," *American Anthropologist,* 58, no. 2 (April 1956): 264–281. See also by the same author *The Death and Rebirth of the Seneca* (New York: Alfred A. Knopf, 1969) and *Religion: An Anthropological View* (New York: Random House, 1965). For an interesting application of Wallace's revitalization model, see William McLoughlin, Jr., *Revivals, Awakenings, and Reform: An Essay on Religion and Social Change in America, 1607–1977* (Chicago: University of Chicago Press, 1978).

16. David F. Noble, *America by Design: Science, Technology, and the Rise of Corporate Capitalism* (New York: Alfred A. Knopf, 1977), xvii.

CHAPTER 2

1. Howard Mumford Jones, *O Strange New World* (New York: Viking, 1964), 1–34.

2. Ibid.

3. Henri Baudet, *Paradise on Earth, Some Thoughts on European Images of Non-European Man,* trans. by Elizabeth Wentholt (New Haven, Conn.: Yale University Press, 1965). Henri Baudet argues that the degree of importance

that paradisiacal quests have is dependent upon the level of ambivalence and the degree of self-satisfaction of any given culture at any given time. If rapid change can be considered a chief promoter of confusion and ambivalence, then Edenic expectations are especially important to understanding American culture because rapid change is a chief characteristic of American history.

4. Jones, *O Strange New World,* 38.

5. Reuben Gold Thwaites, ed., *The Jesuit Relations and Allied Documents,* vol. 47. (Cleveland: Burrows Bros. Co., 1896–1901), 145, 147; Emerson Bennett, *The Renegade* (Cincinnati: Robinson & Jones, 1848). Timothy Flint, *Recollections of the Last Ten Years* (Boston: Cummings, Hilliard, and Co., 1826), 63. See also Arthur K. Moore, *The Frontier Mind* (New York: McGraw-Hill, 1963), 208.

6. James K. Paulding, *The Backwoodsman, A Poem* (Philadelphia: M. Thomas, 1818), 173–174. For a discussion of the changing image of the yeoman farmer, see Henry Nash Smith, *Virgin Land: The American West As Symbol and Myth* (Cambridge, Mass.: Harvard University Press, 1950), 133–134.

7. Smith, *Virgin Land,* 133–134.

8. John Bidwell, *Echoes of the Past* (Chico, Calif.: Chico Advertiser, n.d.), 6.

9. Edwin Bryant, *What I Saw in California* (New York: D. Appleton & Co., 1848) 16–17. For a good discussion of far western imagery, see Ray Allen Billington, *The Far Western Frontier, 1830–1860* (New York: Harper, 1956), 69–90.

10. For a penetrating discussion on manifest destiny and mission, see Frederick Merk, *Manifest Destiny and Mission in American History: A Reinterpretation* (New York: Vintage, 1963). See also Ernest Lee Tuveson, *Redeemer Nation: The Idea of America's Millennial Role* (Chicago: University of Chicago Press, 1968); Also see Norman Cohn, *The Pursuit of the Millennium* (Fairlawn, N.J.: Essential Books, 1957).

11. See Marvin Meyers, *Jacksonian Persuasion: Politics and Belief* (Stanford, Calif.: Stanford University Press, 1957); Edward Pessen, *Jacksonian America: Society, Personality & Politics* (Homewood, Ill.: Dorsey Press, 1978); John William Ward, *Andrew Jackson: Symbol for an Age* (New York: Oxford University Press, 1955); and Arthur M. Schlesinger, *The Age of Jackson* (New York: New American Library, 1945). On legal change, see James Willard Hurst, *Law and the Conditions of Freedom in the Nineteenth-Century United States* (Madison, Wis.: Unversity of Wisconsin Press, 1956); and Morton J. Horowitz, *The Transformation of American Law, 1780–1860* (Cambridge, Mass.: Harvard University Press, 1977).

12. The origins of the themes of concern surrounding political factionalism in the early nineteenth century can be found in Gordon Wood, *The Creation of the American Republic, 1776–1787* (Chapel Hill, N.C.: University of North

Carolina Press, 1969). Also useful is Gerald Stourzh, *Alexander Hamilton and the Idea of Republican Government* (Stanford, Calif.: Stanford University Press, 1970). See also Marshall Smelser, *The Democratic Republic, 1801–1815* (New York: Harper & Row, 1968); and James S. Young, *The Washington Community* (New York: Columbia University Press, 1966).

13. Alexis de Tocqueville, *Democracy in America,* ed. Phillip Bradley (New York: Alfred A. Knopf, 1945), 11. Although Tocqueville was the most perceptive of the European observers, there are numerous accounts of varying quality available. The most useful and widely read are Charles Dickens, *American Notes* (London: Chapman and Hall, 1842); Frances Trollope, *Domestic Manners of the Americans* (London: Whittaker, Treacher & Co., 1832); Michel Chevalier, *Society, Manners and Politics in the United States* (Garden City, N.Y.: Doubleday, 1961); Harriet Martineau, *Society in America,* 2 vols. (London: Saunders & Otley, 1837); Lord James Bryce, *The American Commonwealth* (New York: Macmillan and Co., 1888) Edward Abdy, *Journal of a Residence and Town in the United States,* 3 vols. (London: J. Murray, 1835); Bernhard, Duke of Saxe-Weimar Eisenbach, *Travels Through North America, 1825 and 1826,* 2 vols. (Philadelphia, 1828); John Eyre, *The European Stranger in America* (New York, 1839); Joseph Pickering, *Inquiries of an Emigrant* (London: E. Wilson, 1839). Contemporary scholarly efforts to review European observations of America can be found in Allan Nevins, ed., *America Through British Eyes* (New York: Oxford University Press, 1948); Jane Louise Mesick, *The English Traveller in America, 1785–1835* (New York: Columbia University Press, 1922); Max Berger, *The British Traveler in America, 1836–1860* (New York: Columbia University Press, 1943); Henry Steele Commager, ed., *America in Perspective: The United States Through Foreign Eyes* (New York: Random House, 1947).

14. Samuel Osgood, "The Dark Side of Our National Prosperity," *Western Messenger* (1836): 171, 173, reprinted in David Shi, *In Search of the Simple Life: American Voices, Past and Present* (Salt Lake City: Peregrine Smith Books, 1986), 115. Lyman Beecher, "The Gospel the Only Security for Eminent and Abiding National Prosperity," *American National Preacher* 3 (March 1829), 147, cited in Frederick Somkin, *Unquiet Eagle: Memory and Desire in the Idea of American Freedom, 1815–1860* (Ithaca, N.Y.: Cornell University Press, 1967), 18. See also Lyman Beecher, *A Plea for the West* (Cincinnati: Truman & Smith, 1835).

15. Howard R. Lamar, *Dakota Territory, 1861–1889, A Study of Frontier Politics* (New Haven, Conn.: Yale University Press, 1956), 6–7. For further discussion of disillusionment in the early nineteenth century, see Rowland Berthoff, *Unsettled People: Social Order and Disorder in America* (New York: Harper & Row, 1971); David Rothman, *The Discovery of Asylum: Social Order & Disorder in the New Republic* (Boston: Little Brown, 1971); Alice Felt Tyler, *Freedom's Ferment: Phases of American Social History From the Colonial Period*

to the Outbreak of the Civil War (New York: Harper, 1962). For an urban perspective on early nineteenth-century disillusionment, see Paul Johnson, A Shopkeepers Millennium: Society and Revivals in Rochester, New York, 1815–1837 (New York: Hill and Wang, 1978).

16. Beecher, "The Gospel the Only Security," 147.

17. Berthoff, Unsettled People, 260–263.

18. Ruth Elson, Guardians of Tradition: American School-books of the Nineteenth Century (Lincoln, Nebr.: University of Nebraska Press, 1964), 253, 317.

19. Beecher, "The Gospel the Only Security," 147.

20. Elson, Guardians of Tradition, 223–224.

21. Ibid., 274–276.

22. Ibid., 223–224.

23. Lawrence Cremin, American Education: The National Experience, 1783–1876 (New York: Harper & Row, 1980), 498.

24. Carl Bode, The American Lyceum: Town Meeting of the Mind (New York: Oxford University Press, 1956), 23–26, 31.

25. Stephen Nissenbaum, Sex, Diet and Debility in Jacksonian America: Sylvester Graham and Health Reform (Westport, Conn.: Greenwood Press, 1980), 3–18.

26. Ibid.

27. Ibid., 120.

28. Ibid., 32, 108. See also James C. Whorton, Crusaders for Fitness: A History of American Health Reformers (Princeton, N.J.: Princeton University Press, 1982).

29. John Davies, Phrenology: Fad and Science, A Nineteenth-Century American Crusade (New Haven, Conn.: Yale University Press, 1955), 3-11.

30. Ibid., 50

31. Ibid.

32. Ibid., 157.

33. See Klaus J. Hansen, Mormonism and the American Experience (Chicago: University of Chicago Press, 1981); Thomas O'Dea, The Mormons (Chicago: University of Chicago Press, 1957).

34. Berthoff, Unsettled People, 179–180.

35. Ibid.

36. New Harmony Gazette, July 30, August 6, September 17, October 22, 1828; New Harmony and Nashoba Gazette, or the Free Enquirer, October 29, 1828, cited in Albert Post, Popular Freethought in America, 1825–1850 (New York: Columbia University Press, 1943).

CHAPTER 3

1. Thomas Carlyle, "Sign of the Times," *Edinburgh Review* 49 (June 1829): 439–459.

2. Leo Marx, *The Machine in the Garden: Technology and the Pastoral Eden* (New York: Oxford University Press, 1964), chap. 4.

3. Timothy Walker, "Defence of Mechanical Philosophy," *North American Review* 33 (July 1831): 123.

4. *Scientific American* 5 (Dec. 22, 1849): 109.

5. *Scientific American* 5 (Feb. 23, 1850): 184; Charles Sanford, "The Intellectual Origins and New-Worldliness of American Industry," *Journal of Economic History* 18 (March 1958): 14.

6. For the best source on the early American industrial development, see Marvin Fisher, *Workshops in the Wilderness: The European Response to American Industrialization, 1830–1860* (New York: Oxford University Press, 1967). See also John F. Kasson, *Civilizing the Machine: Technology and Republican Values in America, 1776–1900* (New York: Grossman Publishers, 1976). Also useful is Caroline F. Ware, *The Early New England Cotton Manufacture* (New York: Houghton Mifflin, 1931).

7. *American Journal of Science* 38 (1840): 286.

8. Samuel F.B. Morse,"Examination of the Telegraphic Apparatus and the Processes in Telegraphy," in William P. Blake, *Report of the United States Commissioner on the Paris Universal Exposition, 1867,* vol. 3 (Washington, D.C.: U.S. Government Printing Office, 1867) 50. "Modern Science," *Scientific American* 3 (Jan. 22, 1848): 67.

9. *Scientific American* (Sept. 4, 1847): 397; *Scientific American* 2 (March 1860) (new series): 216; James T. Austin, *Address Delivered Before the Massachusetts Charitable Mechanics Association* (Boston: The Association, 1839); *American Artisan and Patent Record* 1 (May 10, 1865): 2.

10. Edward Riddle, *Report on the World's Exposition,* Report of the Commissioner of Patents for the Year 1851, 32d Cong., 1st sess. H. Exec. Doc. 102, pt. 1, 484–485.

11. Ibid.

12. "Civilization, Inventors, Invention and the Arts," *Scientific American* 5 (Feb. 16, 1850): 173. *Scientific American* 5 (May 25, 1850): 285.

13. Quotes taken from Fisher, *Workshops in the Wilderness,* 72–73.

14. Between 1877 and 1890, railroad mileage increased from 79,082 miles of track to 166,703 miles of track. By the turn of the century, U.S. steel production surpassed that of both Great Britain and Germany, the world's two leading steel producers. Because of the rapid rate of urbanization,

lumber production increased from 12.7 million board feet to 27 million board feet during this period.

15. Francis Bowen, *American Political Economy* (New York: Charles Scribner & Co., 1870); John Whiteclay Chambers, *The Tyranny of Change: America in the Progressive Era, 1900–1917* (New York: St. Martin's Press, 1980), 1–6.

16. For general information on industrial and agricultural expansion, see John A. Garraty, *The New Commonwealth, 1877–1890* (New York: Harper & Row, 1968); and Chambers, *The Tyranny of Change*. See also Samuel P. Hays, *The Response to Industrialism, 1885–1914* (Chicago: University of Chicago Press, 1957); and Thomas C. Cochran and William Miller, *The Age of Enterprise: A Social History of Industrial America* (New York: Macmillan, 1942).

17. The most insightful book on populism is Lawrence Goodwyn, *Democratic Promise: The Populist Movement in America* (New York: Oxford University Press, 1976). See also John D. Hicks, *The Populist Revolt* (Minneapolis: University of Minnesota Press, 1931); Norman Pollack, *The Populist Response to Industrial America* (Cambridge, Mass.: Harvard University Press, 1962) and Walter T.K. Nugent, *The Tolerant Populists: Kansas Populism and Nativism* (Chicago: University of Chicago Press, 1963).

18. Merger statistics taken from Howard N. Ross, "Economic Growth and Change in the United States Under Laisse Faire: 1870–1929," in Frederick Cople Jaher, ed., *The Age of Industrialism in America: Essays in Social Structure and Cultural Values* (New York: Free Press, 1968), 41. The most important book on business patterns during this period is Alfred Chandler, Jr., *The Visible Hand: The Managerial Revolution in American Business* (Cambridge, Mass.: Belknap Press, 1977. See also Glenn Porter and H. C. Livesay, *Merchants and Manufacturers: Studies in the Changing Structure of Nineteenth Century Marketing* (Baltimore: Johns Hopkins Press, 1971); Glenn Porter, *The Rise of Big Business, 1860–1910* (New York: Thomas Crowell, 1973) and E. C. Kirkland, *Industry Comes of Age: Business, Labor, and Public Policy, 1860-1897* (Chicago: Quadrangle Books, 1967).

19. Urbanization statistics taken from Garraty, *The New Commonwealth*, 179–180. See also Alan Trachtenberg, *The Incorporation of America: Culture and Society in the Gilded Age* (New York: Hill and Wang, 1982); Blake McKelvey, *The Urbanization of America, 1860–1915* (New Brunswick, N.J.: Rutgers University Press, 1963) and *The Emergence of Metropolitan America, 1915–1966* (New Brunswick, N.J.: Rutgers University Press, 1968); and Constance McLaughlin, *American Cities in the Growth of the Nation* (New York: J. DeGraff, 1957).

20. Immigrant data taken from Michael Parenti, "Immigration and Political Life," in Jaher, ed., *The Age of Industrialism*, 81. See also John Higham, *Strangers in the Land* (New Brunswick, N.J.: Rutgers University Press, 1955); Oscar Handlin, *The Uprooted* (New York: Grosset & Dunlap, 1951); Philip Taylor, *The Distant Magnet: European Emigration to the U.S.A.* (New York:

Harper & Row, 1971); and Maldwyn A. Jones, *American Immigration* (Chicago: University of Chicago Press, 1960).

21. Frederick Lewis Allen, *The Big Change: America Transforms Itself, 1900–1950* (New York: Harper, 1952), 57; Robert Hunter, *Poverty* (New York: Macmillan, 1904).

22. Ibid.; Jacob A. Riis, *The Battle With the Slum* (New York: Macmillan, 1902), 95, 118–120. See also Riis's classic, *How the Other Half Lives* (New York: Hill and Wang, 1957).

23. Robert Wiebe, *The Search for Order, 1877–1890* (New York: Hill and Wang, 1967), 1–43.

24. Lawrence Cremin, *The Transformation of the School: Progressivism in American Education, 1876–1957* (New York: Alfred A. Knopf, 1961), 121–122.

25. Ibid.

26. Cremin, *The Transformation of the School,* 117, 109. See also William James, *Pragmatism* (New York: Longmans, Green and Co., 1907) and *The Meaning of Truth* (New York: Longmans, Green and Co., 1909).

27. Cremin, *The Transformation of the School,* 115–126. See also John Dewey, *The School and Society* (Chicago: University of Chicago Press, 1899) and *Democracy and Education* (New York: Macmillan, 1916).

28. See Louis Filler, *The Muckrakers* (University Park, Pa.: Penn State University Press, 1976).

29. See Victoria Case and Robert Ormond Case, *We Called It Culture: The Story of the Chautauqua* (Garden City, N.Y.: Doubleday, 1948).

30. James H. Timberlake, *Prohibition and the Progressive Movement, 1900–1920* (Cambridge, Mass.: Harvard University Press, 1963), 52–53.

31. Ibid., 67–69.

32. Quoted in H. Wayne Morgan, *Yesterday's Addicts: American Society and Drug Abuse, 1865–1920* (Norman, Okla.: University of Oklahoma Press, 1974), 18.

33. See George Beard, *American Nervousness: Its Causes and Consequences* (New York: G. P. Putnam, 1881), 64. Quoted in Morgan, *Yesterday's Addicts,* 8. See also Donald Meyer, *The Positive Thinkers: Religion As Pop Psychology From Mary Baker Eddy to Oral Roberts* (New York: Pantheon Books, 1980).

34. H. Wayne Morgan, *Drugs in America: A Social History, 1800–1980* (Syracuse, N.Y.: Syracuse University Press, 1981), 94–96.

35. James C. Whorton, *Crusaders for Fitness: The History of American Health Reformers* (Princeton, N.J.: Princeton University Press, 1982), 168–200.

36. Ibid., 215.

37. Ibid., 204.

38. "Don't Let Your Great-Great Grandmother Tell You What to Eat!" *Ladies Home Journal* 42 (Dec. 1925), quoted in Paul A. Carter, *Another Part of the Twenties* (New York: Columbia University Press, 1977), 137.

39. "The Survival of the Fittest," *Saturday Evening Post* 198 (July 3, 1926), taken from Carter, *Another Part of the Twenties,* 140–141.

40. Whorton, *Crusaders for Fitness,* 296–304.

41. Ibid., 273–274.

42. Ibid., 304–330.

43. Ibid., 281.

44. See Cynthia Eagle Russett, *Darwin in America: The Intellectual Response, 1865–1912* (San Francisco: W. H. Freeman, 1976); Robert Bannister, *Social Darwinism: Science and Myth in Anglo-American Social Thought* (Philadelphia: Temple University Press, 1979); and Richard Hofstadter, *Social Darwinism in American Thought: 1860–1915* (Philadelphia: University of Pennsylvania Press, 1945). Roderick Nash, *The Nervous Generation: American Thought, 1917–1930* (Chicago: Elephant Paperbacks, 1990); Stow Persons, *American Minds: A History of Ideas* (New York: Holt, Rinehart & Winston, 1958); Frederick J. Hoffman, *The Twenties: American Writing in the Postwar Decade,* rev. ed. (New York: Viking Press, 1962); and Morton G. White, *Social Thought in America: The Revolt Against Formalism* (New York: Viking Press, 1949).

45. Mark Haller, *Eugenics: Hereditarian Attitudes in American Thought* (New Brunswick, N.J.: Rutgers University Press, 1963), 3–7. See also Donald Pickens, *Eugenics and the Progressives* (Nashville: Vanderbilt University Press, 1968).

46. Madison Grant, *The Passing of the Great Race* (New York: Charles Scribner's Sons, 1918), 12.

47. Lothrop Stoddard, *The Rising Tide of Color* (New York: Charles Scribner's Sons, 1920), 302.

48. See Robert K. Murray, *The Red Scare: A Study in National Hysteria* (Minneapolis: University of Minnesota Press, 1955), 256–257; and Stanley Coben, *A. Mitchell Palmer: Politician* (New York: Columbia University Press, 1963).

49. George E. Mowrey, *The Twenties: Fords, Flappers & Fanatics* (Englewood Cliffs, N.J.: Prentice-Hall, 1963), 137.

50. Quoted in Clyde Griffen, "The Progressive Ethos," in Stanley Coben and Lorman Ratner, eds., *The Development of American Culture* (New York: St Martin's Press, 1973), 153. Many insights into the transformation of popular culture can be gained from Paula Fass, *The Damned and the Beautiful: American Youth in the 1920s* (New York: Oxford University Press, 1977). See also Robert Crunden, *From Self to Society: Transition in American Thought, 1919–1941* (Englewood Cliffs, N.J.: Prentice-Hall, 1972).

CHAPTER 4

1. Henry George, *Progress and Poverty* (New York: H. George, 1888). Quote taken from Robert H. Wiebe, *The Search for Order* (New York: Hill and Wang, 1967), 138. See also the introduction in Edward Bellamy, *Looking Backward, 2000–1887,* ed. John Thomas (Cambridge, Mass.: Harvard University Press, Belknap Press, 1967).

2. Ralph Henry Gabriel, *The Course of American Democratic Thought* (New York: Ronald Press Co., 1956), 248.

3. Herbert Croly, *The Promise of American Life* (Hamden, Conn.: Archon Books, 1909). Croly quotes taken from David W. Levy, *Herbert Croly of the New Republic* (Princeton, N.J.: Princeton University Press, 1985), 97, 110, 115–116.

4. Levy, *Herbert Croly of the New Republic,* 96–131.

5. Material taken from Samuel Haber, *Efficiency and Uplift: Scientific Management in the Progressive Era, 1890–1920* (Chicago: University of Chicago Press, 1964), 59–64. Frederick Taylor, *Principles of Scientific Management* (New York: Harper & Brothers, 1911). See also Daniel Nelson, *Frederick W. Taylor and the Rise of Scientific Management* (Madison, Wis.: University of Wisconsin Press, 1980); and Howard Segal, *Technological Utopianism in American Culture* (Chicago: University of Chicago Press, 1985), 98–128.

6. Haber, *Efficiency and Uplift,* 59–64.

7. Ibid. For an interesting discussion of Bruce Barton, see T. Jackson Lears, "From Salvation to Self-Realization: Advertising and the Therapeutic Roots of the Consumer Culture, 1880–1930," in Richard Wightman Fox and T. Jackson Lears, eds., *The Culture of Consumption: Critical Essays in American History, 1880–1980* (New York: Pantheon Books, 1983).

8. Haber, *Efficiency and Uplift,* 59–64.

9. Otis L. Graham, Jr., "The Planning Idea and American Reality: 1930s," in Stanley Elkins and Eric McKitrick, eds., *The Hofstadter Aegis: A Memorial* (New York: Alfred A. Knopf, 1974), 262. Segal, *Technological Utopianism in American Culture,* 111.

10. Graham, "The Planning Idea and American Reality," 262. See also Otis L. Graham, Jr., *Toward a Planned Society: From Roosevelt to Nixon* (New York: Oxford University Press, 1976).

11. David Riesman, "From Morality to Morale," in Alfred H. Stanton and Stewart E. Perry, eds., *Personality and Political Crisis: New Perspectives From Social Science and Psychiatry for the Study of War and Politics* (Glencoe, Ill.: Free Press, 1951), 83–42. This essay is a succinct discussion of themes elaborated on in Riesman's *The Lonely Crowd* (New Haven, Conn.: Yale University Press, 1950). For a penetrating discussion of the late nineteenth-century origins of the consumer culture and its many ramifications, see T. Jackson

Lears, *No Place of Grace: Antimodernism and the Transformation of American Culture, 1880–1920* (New York: Pantheon, 1981).

12. William Whyte, *The Organization Man* (Garden City, N.Y.: Doubleday, 1956), 6; Paul Goodman, *Growing Up Absurd* (New York: Random House, 1960), 12.

13. Reprinted in Thomas Parkinton, *A Casebook on the Beat* (New York: Crowell, 1961), 26–27. For additional works on the beat writers, see John Tytell, *Naked Angels: The Lives and Literature of the Beat Generation* (New York: McGraw-Hill, 1976); and Bruce Cook, *The Beat Generation* (New York: Scribner, 1971).

14. See note 13.

15. Timothy Leary, *The Politics of Ecstasy* (New York: Putnam, 1968), 162–163.

16. Paul Jacobs and Sol Landau, eds., *The New Radicals: A Report with Documents* (New York: Random House, 1966), 154. See also Theodore Roszak, *The Making of a Counterculture* (Garden City, N.Y.: Doubleday, 1969); Philip Slater, *The Pursuit of Loneliness* (Boston: Beacon, 1970); Ronald Berman, *America in the Sixties: An Intellectual History* (New York: Free Press, 1968); Morris Dickstein, *Gates of Eden: American Culture in the Sixties* (New York: Basic Books, 1977); and Peter Clecak, *America's Quest for the Ideal Self: Dissent and Fulfillment in the 60s and 70s* (New York: Oxford University Press, 1983). For the middle-class response to the counterrevolution, see Richard Lemon, *The Troubled American* (New York: Simon and Schuster, 1970); Murray Friedman, ed., *Overcoming Middle Class Rage* (Philadelphia: Westminster Press, 1971); and Louise K. Howe, ed., *The White Majority: Between Poverty and Affluence* (New York: Vintage Books, 1971).

17. See Gregory Johnson, "The Hare Krishna in San Francisco," in Charles Y. Glock and Robert N. Bellah, eds., *The New Religious Consciousness* (Berkeley, Calif.: University of California Press, 1976), 31–51; and Alan Tobey, "The Summer Solstice of the Healthy-Happy-Holy Organization," in Glock and Bellah, eds., *New Religious Consciousness*, 5–30; *Newsweek* (March 22, 1971): 97.

18. Albert Bergensen and Mark Warr, "A Crisis in Moral Order: The Effects of Watergate Upon the Confidence in Social Institutions," in Robert Wuthnow, ed., *The Religious Dimension: New Directions in Quantitative Research* (New York: Academic Press, 1979) 284–288; and Daniel Yankelovich, *New Rules: Searching for Self-Fulfillment in a World Turned Upside Down* (New York: Random House, 1981), 12.

19. *Newsweek* (March 22, 1971): 97.

20. Yankelovich, *New Rules*, 184–185; *The Connecticut Mutual Life Report on American Values in the 80s* (Hartford, Conn.: Connecticut Mutual Life Insurance Co., 1981), 19.

21. Diane Ravitch, *The Troubled Crusade: American Education, 1945–1980* (New York: Basic Books, 1983), 70–73. See also Lawrence Cremin, *The Transfor-*

mation of the School : Progressivism in American Education, 1876–1957 (New York: Alfred A. Knopf, 1961).

22. Ravitch, *The Troubled Crusade,* 79. For an additional perspective on educational experimentation see Paula Fass, *Outside In: Minorities and the Transformation of American Education* (New York: Oxford University Press, 1989).

23. National Commission on Excellence in Education, "A Nation at Risk" (Washington, D.C., 1983), 8–10. See also "Libraries and the Learning Society," in *Papers in Response to a Nation at Risk* (Chicago: American Library Association, 1984).

24. See note 23.

25. William Bennett, "James Madison High School," (Washington, D.C.: U.S. Department. of Education, 1987) and "James Madison Elementary School,"(Washington, D.C.: U.S. Department of Education, 1988).

26. Yankelovich, *New Rules,* 62.

27. Donald Stone, "The Human Potential Movement," in Glock and Bellah, eds., *New Religious Consciousness,* 93, 112.

28. Peter Marin, "The New Narcissism," *Harper's* 251 (October 1975): 46.

29. Stone, "The Human Potential Movement," 94; Abraham Maslow, *The Farther Reaches of Human Nature* (New York: Viking Press, 1970), 158.

30. Robert J. Ringer, *Looking Out for Number One* (New York: Funk & Wagnalls, 1977); George Weinberg, *Self Creation* (New York: Avon, 1979); Wayne Dyer, *Your Erroneous Zones* (New York: Funk & Wagnalls, 1977) and *Pulling Your Own Strings* (New York: T. Y. Crowell, 1979); Harry Browne, *How I Found Freedom in an Unfree World* (New York: Macmillan, 1974); Harold S. Kushner, *When All You've Ever Wanted Isn't Enough* (New York: Pan, 1986); Mildred Newman and Bernard Berkowitz, *How to Be Your Own Best Friend* (New York: Ballantine, 1981).

31. *Time* 118 (November 2, 1981): 95; *Time* 126 (October 7, 1985): 60–61; *Time* 127 (June 16, 1986): 77; *Time* 131 (July 25, 1988): 66–67.

32. Quotes taken from *Time* 131 (July 25, 1988): 66–67. See also Arthur J. Barsky, *Worried Sick: Our Troubled Quest for Wellness* (Boston: Little Brown, 1988); and Barry Glassner, *Bodies: Why We Look the Way We Do (And How We Feel About It)* (New York: Putnam, 1988). The *American Health* quote taken from a billboard at the YMCA in Norman, Oklahoma.

33. *Time* 131 (July 25, 1988): 66–67.

34. For discussions of the conservative trends, see Allan Crawford, *Thunder on the Right: The New Right and the Politics of Resentment* (New York: Pantheon, 1980); and George Nash, *The Conservative Intellectual Movement in America* (New York: Basic Books, 1976).

CHAPTER 5

1. Arthur C. Clarke, *1984: Spring, A Choice of Futures* (New York: Ballantine Books, 1984), 69–70. See also J. Bonner and J. Weir, *The Next Hundred Years* (New York: Viking Press, 1957); Victor Ferkiss, *Futurology: Promise Performance, Prospects* (Beverly Hills, Calif.: Sage Publications, 1977); and H. Kahn, W. Brown, and L. Martel, *The Next 200 Years* (New York: William Morrow, 1976).

2. Carl R. Rogers, "Communities," in Alberto Villoldo and Ken Dychtwald, eds., *Millennium: Glimpses Into the 21st Century* (Boston: Houghton Mifflin, 1981), 145.

3. James Martin, *Viewdata and the Information Society* (Englewood Cliffs, N.J.: Prentice-Hall, 1982), 137.

4. Loy A. Singleton, *Telecommunication in the Information Age: A Nontechnical Primer on the New Technologies* (Cambridge, Mass.: Ballinger Pub. Co., 1983), 197. See also Alvin Toffler, *The Third Wave* (New York: William Morrow, 1980).

5. Timothy Walker, "Defence of Mechanical Philosophy," *North American Review* 33 (July 1831): 123. Samuel F.B. Morse, "Examination of the Telegraphic Apparatus and the Processes in Telegraphy," in William P. Blake, *Report of the United States Commissioner on the Paris Universal Exposition, 1867*, vol. 3 (Washington, D.C.: U.S. Government Printing Office, 1867), 50.

6. Marvin Cetron and Thomas O'Toole, *Encounters With the Future: A Forecast of Life Into the 21st Century* (New York: McGraw-Hill, 1982), 233–251.

7. Ibid., 248.

8. G. Harry Stine, *The Hopeful Future* (New York: Macmillan, 1983), 125, 138.

9. Ibid.

10. Timothy Leary, "Science," in Villoldo and Dychtwald, eds., *Millennium*, 291. See also Bernard D. Davis, "The Recombinant DNA Scenarios: Andromeda Strain, Chimera, and Golem," *American Scientist* 65 (1977).

11. *American Polytechnic Journal* 2 (1853): 160; *American Journal of Science* 38 (1840): 286.

12. Gerard K. O'Neill, *The High Frontier: Human Colonies in Space* (New York: Morrow, 1977), 36–37. See also Dandridge M. Cole and Roy G. Scarfo, *Beyond Tomorrow* (Amherst, Wis.: Amherst Press, 1965); Dandridge M. Cole and Donald William Cox, *Islands in Space* (New York: Chilton Books, 1964); J. Billingham and W. Gilbrath, eds., *Space Resources and Space Settlements*, NASA SP-428 (Washington, D.C., 1979); Konstantin Tsiolkowski, *Beyond the Planet Earth* (New York: Pergamon Press, 1960); P. J. Vajk, "The Impact of Space Colonization on World Dynamics," *Technological Forecasting and Social Change* 9 (1976).

13. Gerard K. O'Neill, *2081: A Hopeful View of the Human Future* (New York: Simon & Schuster, 1981), 74.

14. Sinclair Lewis, *Main Street* (New York: Harcourt, Brace & World, 1948), 265.

15. Arthur K. Moore, *The Frontier Mind* (New York: McGraw-Hill, 1963), 208; *Scientific American* 5 (Feb. 16, 1850): 173.

EPILOGUE

1. Stuart Bruchey, *The Wealth of the Nation: An Economic History of the United States.* (New York: Harper & Row, 1988), 198–199, 207–211.

2. Ibid.

3. Alan Pifer and Lydia Bronte, eds., *Our Aging Society: Paradox and Promise* (New York: W. W. Norton, 1986), 1–13; See also Landon Y. Jones, *Great Expectations: America and the Baby Boom Generation* (New York: Coward, McCann & Geoghegan, 1980); and Kevin Phillips, *The Politics of the Rich and the Poor* (New York, Coward, McCann & Geoghegan, 1990).

4. Pifer and Bronte, *Our Aging Society,* 1–13.

5. Paul E. Zopf, Jr., *America's Older Population* (Houston: Cap and Gown Press, 1986), 291–292.

6. Malcolm Morrison, "Work and Retirement in an Older Society," in Pifer and Bronte, eds., *Our Aging Society,* 342–343.

7. David Levy, *Herbert Croly of the New Republic* (Princeton, N.J.: Princeton University Press, 1985), 97,110, 115–116. Howard N. Ross, "Economic Growth and Change in the United States under laissez faire: 1870-1929," in Frederick Cople Jaher, ed., *The Age of Industrialism in America: Essays in Social Structure and Cultural Values* (New York: Free Press, 1968), 6–42. See also John Chambers, *The Tyranny of Change: America in the Progressive Era, 1900-1917* (New York: St. Martin's Press, 1980), 73–-04.

8. Bruchey, *The Wealth of the Nation,* 220–221.

9. Post–World War II statistics taken from U.S. Bureau of the Census, "Money Income in 1974 of Families and Persons in the United States," *Current Population Reports,* series P-60, no. 101, table 22, p. 37. See also Harrell R. Rodgers, Jr., *Poverty Amid Plenty: A Political and Economic Analysis* (Reading, Mass.: Addison-Wesley Co., 1979), 17–40.

Bibliography ❧

BOOKS

Abdy, Edward S. *Journal of a Residence and Town in the United States.* 3 vols. London: J. Murray, 1835.

Allen, Frederick Lewis. *The Big Change: America Transforms Itself, 1900–1950.* New York: Harper, 1952.

Austin, James T. *Address Delivered Before the Massachusetts Charitable Mechanics Association.* Boston: The Association, 1839.

Bailyn, Bernard. *The Ideological Origins of the American Revolution.* Cambridge, Mass.: Harvard University Press, 1971.

Bannister, Robert. *Social Darwinism: Science and Myth in Anglo-American Social Thought.* Philadelphia: Temple University Press, 1979.

Barsky, Arthur J. *Worried Sick: Our Troubled Quest for Wellness.* Boston: Little Brown, 1988.

Barth, Gunther. *City People: The Rise of Modern City Culture in Nineteenth Century America.* New York: Oxford University Press, 1980.

Barton, Bruce. *The Man Nobody Knows.* Indianapolis: The Bobbs-Merrill Co., 1925.

Baudet, Henri. *Paradise on Earth: Some Thoughts on European Images of Non-European Man.* Translated by Elizabeth Wentholt. New Haven, Conn.: Yale University Press, 1965.

Beard, George. *American Nervousness: Its Causes and Consequences.* New York: G. P. Putnam, 1881.

Beecher, Lyman. *A Plea for the West.* Cincinnati: Truman & Smith, 1835.

Bellamy, Edward. *Looking Backward: 2000–1887.* Boston: Houghton Mifflin, 1887.

Bennett, Emerson. *The Renegade.* Cincinnati: Robinson & Jones, 1848.

Bennett, William. "James Madison High School." Washington D.C.: U.S. Department of Education, 1987.

———. "James Madison Elementary School." Washington D.C.: U.S. Department of Education, 1988.

Bercovitch, Sacvan. *The American Jeremiad.* Madison: University of Wisconsin Press, 1978.

Berger, Max. *The British Traveller in America, 1836–1860.* New York: Columbia University Press, 1943.

Berman, Ronald. *America in the Sixties: An Intellectual History.* New York: Free Press, 1968.

Berthoff, Rowland. *An Unsettled People: Social Order and Disorder in America.* New York: Harper & Row, 1971.

Bidwell, John. *Echoes of the Past About California.* Chico, Calif.: Chico Advertiser, n.d.

Billingham, J., and W. Gilbrath, eds. *Space Resources and Space Settlements,* NASA SP-428. Washington, D.C., 1979.

Billington, Ray Allen. *America's Frontier Heritage.* New York: Holt, Rinehart and Winston, 1966.

———. *The Far Western Frontier, 1830–1860.* New York: Harper, 1956.

Blake, William P. *Report of the United States Commissioner on the Paris Universal Exposition, 1867.* 6 vols. Washington, D.C.: U.S. Government Printing Office, 1867.

Bode, Carl. *The American Lyceum: Town Meeting of the Mind.* New York: Oxford University Press, 1956.

Bonner, J., and J. Weir. *The Next Hundred Years.* New York: Viking Press, 1957.

Bowen, Francis. *American Political Economy.* New York: Charles Scribner & Co., 1870.

Bruchey, Stuart. *The Roots of American Economic Growth, 1607–1861: An Essay in Social Causation.* New York: Harper & Row, 1965.

———. *The Wealth of the Nation: An Economic History of the United States.* New York: Harper & Row, 1988.

Bryant, Edwin. *What I Saw in California.* New York: D. Appleton & Co., 1848.

Bryce, James. *The American Commonwealth.* 2 vols. New York: Macmillan, 1888.

Carter, Paul A. *Another Part of the Twenties.* New York: Columbia University Press, 1977.

Case, Victoria, and Robert Ormond Case. *We Called It Culture: The Story of the Chautauqua.* Garden City, N.Y.: Doubleday, 1948.

Cetron, Marvin, and Thomas O'Toole. *Encounters With the Future: A Forecast of Life Into the 21st Century.* New York: McGraw-Hill, 1982.

Chambers, John Whiteclay, II. *The Tyranny of Change: America in the Progressive Era, 1900–1917.* New York: St. Martin's Press, 1980.

Chandler, Alfred D., Jr., *The Visible Hand: The Managerial Revolution in American Business.* Cambridge, Mass.: Belknap Press, 1977.

Chevalier, Michel. *Society, Manners and Politics in the United States.* Garden City, N.Y.: Doubleday, 1961.

Clarke, Arthur C. *1984: Spring, A Choice of Futures.* New York: Ballantine Books, 1984.

———. *Profiles of the Future: An Inquiry into the Limits of the Possible.* New York: Holt, Rinehart and Winston, 1984.

Clecak, Peter. *America's Quest for the Ideal Self: Dissent and Fulfillment in the 60s and 70s.* New York: Oxford University Press, 1983.

Coben, Stanley. *A. Mitchell Palmer: Politician.* New York: Columbia University Press, 1963.

Coben, Stanley, and Lorman Ratner, eds. *The Development of American Culture.* New York: St. Martin's Press, 1970.

Cochran, Thomas C., and William Miller. *The Age of Enterprise: A Social History of Industrial America.* New York: Macmillan, 1942.

Cohn, Norman. *The Pursuit of the Millennium.* Fairlawn, N.J.: Essential Books, 1957.

Cole, Dandridge M., and Donald William Cox. *Islands in Space.* New York: Chilton Books, 1964.

Cole, Dandridge M., and Roy G. Scarfo. *Beyond Tomorrow.* Amherst, Wis.: Amherst Press, 1965.

Commager, Henry Steele, ed. *America in Perspective: The United States Through Foreign Eyes.* New York: Random House, 1947.

Connecticut Mutual Life Report on American Values in the 80s. Hartford, Conn.: Connecticut Mutual Life Insurance Co., 1981.

Conwell, Russell. *Acres of Diamonds.* New York: Harper and Brothers, 1915.

Cook, Bruce. *The Beat Generation.* New York: Scribner, 1971.

Crawford, Allan. *Thunder on the Right: The New Right and the Politics of Resentment.* New York: Pantheon, 1980.

Cremin, Lawrence. *The Transformation of the School: Progressivism in American Education, 1876-1957.* New York: Alfred A. Knopf, 1961.

Croly, Herbert. *The Promise of American Life.* Hamden, Conn.: Archon Books, 1909.

Crunden, Robert. *From Self to Society: Transition in American Thought, 1919-1941.* Englewood Cliffs, N.J.: Prentice-Hall, 1972.

Davies, John. *Phrenology: Fad and Science, A Nineteenth-Century American Crusade.* New Haven, Conn.: Yale University Press, 1955.

Dewey, John. *Democracy and Education.* New York: Macmillan, 1916.

———. *The School and Society.* Chicago: University of Chicago Press, 1899.

Dickens, Charles. *American Notes.* London: Chapman and Hall, 1842.

Dickstein, Morris. *Gates of Eden: American Culture in the Sixties.* New York: Basic Books, 1977.

Ekrich, Arthur. *The Idea of Progress in America, 1815–1860.* New York: Columbia University Press, 1944.

Elbert, Donald, and Stow Persons, eds. *Socialism and American Life.* 2 vols. Princeton, N.J.: Princeton University Press, 1952.

Elkins, Stanley, and Eric McKitrick, eds. *The Hofstadter Aegis: A Memorial.* New York: Alfred A. Knopf, 1974.

Elson, Ruth. *Guardians of Tradition: American Schoolbooks of the Nineteenth Century.* Lincoln, Nebr.: University of Nebraska Press, 1964.

Eyre, John. *The European Stranger in America.* New York, 1839.

Fass, Paula. *The Damned and the Beautiful: American Youth in the 1920s.* New York: Oxford University Press, 1977.

———. *Outside In: Minorities and the Transformation of American Education.* New York: Oxford University Press, 1989.

Ferkiss, Victor. *Futurology: Promise, Performance, Prospects.* Beverly Hills, Calif.: Sage Publications, 1977.

Filler, Louis. *The Muckrakers.* University Park, Pa.: Penn State University Press, 1976.

Fine, Sidney. *Laissez-Faire and the General Welfare State: A Study of Conflict in American Thought, 1865–1901.* Ann Arbor, Mich.: University of Michigan Press, 1956.

Fisher, Marvin. *Workshops in the Wilderness: The European Response to American Industrialization, 1830–1860.* New York: Oxford University Press, 1967.

Flint, Timothy. *Recollections of the Last Ten Years.* Boston: Cummings, Hilliard and Co., 1826.

Fox, Richard Wightman, and T. Jackson Lears, eds. *The Culture of Consumption: Critical Essays in American History, 1880–1980.* New York: Pantheon Books, 1983.

Frampton, John. *Joyful Newes Out of the Newe Founde World.* London: Constable and Co., Ltd., 1588.

Friedman, Murray, ed. *Overcoming Middle Class Rage.* Philadelphia: Westminster Press, 1971.

Gabriel, Ralph Henry. *The Course of American Democratic Thought.* New York: Ronald Press Co., 1956.

Garraty, John A. *The New Commonwealth, 1877–1890.* New York: Harper & Row, 1968.

George, Henry. *Progress and Poverty.* New York: H. George, 1879.

Gladden, Washington. *Social Salvation.* Boston: Houghton Mifflin, 1902.

Glassner, Barry. *Bodies: Why We Look the Way We Do (And How We Feel About It)*. New York: Putnam, 1988.

Glock, Charles Y., and Robert N. Bellah, eds. *The New Religious Consciousness*. Berkeley, Calif: University of California Press, 1976.

Gold Thwaites, Reuben, ed. *The Jesuit Relations and Allied Documents*, vol. 47. Cleveland: Burrows Bros. Co., 1896–1901.

Goodman, Paul. *Growing Up Absurd*. New York: Random House, 1960.

Goodwyn, Lawrence. *Democratic Promise: The Populist Movement in America*. New York: Oxford University Press, 1976.

Graham, Otis L., Jr. *Toward a Planned Society: From Roosevelt to Nixon*. New York: Oxford University Press, 1976.

Grant, Madison. *The Passing of the Great Race*. New York: Charles Scribner's Sons, 1918.

Green, Constance McLaughlin. *American Cities in the Building of the Nation*. New York: J. DeGraff, 1956.

Haber, Samuel. *Efficiency and Uplift: Scientific Management in the Progressive Era, 1890–1920*. Chicago: University of Chicago Press, 1964.

Haller, Mark H. *Eugenics: Hereditarian Attitudes in American Thought*. New Brunswick, N.J.: Rutgers University Press, 1963.

Handlin, Oscar. *The Uprooted*. New York: Grosset & Dunlap, 1951.

Hansen, Klaus J. *Mormonism and the American Experience*. Chicago: University of Chicago Press, 1981.

Hays, Samuel P. *The Response to Industrialism, 1885–1914*. Chicago: University of Chicago Press, 1957.

Hicks, John D. *The Populist Revolt*. Minneapolis: University of Minnesota Press, 1931.

Higham, John. *Strangers in the Land*. New Brunswick, N.J.: Rutgers University Press, 1955.

Hoffman, Frederick J. *The Twenties: American Writing in the Postwar Decade*. Rev. ed. New York: Viking Press, 1962.

Hofstadter, Richard. *Social Darwinism in American Thought, 1860–1915*. Philadelphia: University of Pennsylvania Press, 1945.

Horowitz, Morton J. *The Transformation of American Law, 1780–1860*. Cambridge, Mass.: Harvard University Press, 1977.

Howe, Louise K., ed. *The White Majority: Between Poverty and Affluence*. New York: Vintage Books, 1971.

Hughes, Thomas Parke. *Changing Attitudes Toward American Technology*. New York: Viking, 1975.

Hurst, James Willard. *Law and the Conditions of Freedom in the Nineteenth-Century United States*. Madison, Wis.: University of Wisconsin Press, 1956.

Israel, Jerry, ed. *Building the Organizational Society: Essays on Associational Activities in Modern America.* New York: Free Press, 1972.

Jacobs, Paul, and Sol Landau, eds. *The New Radicals: A Report With Documents.* New York: Random House, 1966.

Jaher, Frederic Cople, ed. *The Age of Industrialism in America: Essays in Social Structure and Cultural Values.* New York: Free Press, 1968.

James, William. *Pragmatism.* New York: Longmans, Green and Co., 1907.

———. *The Meaning of Truth.* New York: Longmans, Green and Co., 1909.

Johnson, Paul E. *A Shopkeepers Millennium: Society and Revivals in Rochester, New York, 1815–1837.* New York: Hill and Wang, 1978.

Jones, Howard Mumford. *O Strange New World.* New York: Viking, 1964.

Jones, Landon Y. *Great Expectations: America and the Baby Boom Generation.* New York: Coward, McCann & Geoghegan, 1980.

Jones, Maldwyn A. *American Immigration.* Chicago: University of Chicago Press, 1960.

Kahn, Herman, W. Brown, and Leon Martel. *The Next 200 Years.* New York: William Morrow, 1976.

Kasson, John F. *Civilizing the Machine: Technology and Republican Values in America, 1776–1900.* New York: Grossman Publishers, 1976.

Katz, Michael B. *The Irony of Early School Reform: Educational Innovation in the Mid-Nineteenth Century Massachusetts.* Cambridge, Mass.: Harvard University Press, 1968.

Kirkland, Edward Chase. *Industry Comes of Age: Business, Labor, and Public Policy, 1860–1897.* Chicago: Quadrangle Books, 1967.

Lamar, Howard R. *Dakota Territory, 1861–1889: A Study of Frontier Politics.* New Haven, Conn.: Yale University Press, 1956.

Lasch, Christopher. *The Culture of Narcissism: The Problems of Youth in the Organized Society.* New York: W. W. Norton, 1978.

Laslett, Peter. *The World We Have Lost.* London: Methuen, 1965.

Lears, T. Jackson. *No Place of Grace: Antimodernism and the Transformation of American Culture, 1880–1920.* New York: Pantheon, 1981.

Leary, Timothy. *The Politics of Ecstasy.* New York: G. P. Putnam, 1968.

Lemon, Richard. *The Troubled American.* New York: Simon & Schuster, 1970.

Levy, David W. *Herbert Croly of the New Republic.* Princeton, N.J.: Princeton University Press, 1985.

Lincoln, Bruce. *Discourse and the Construction of Society.* New York: Oxford University Press, 1989.

McKelvey, Blake. *The Emergence of Metropolitan America, 1915–1966.* New Brunswick, N.J.: Rutgers University Press, 1968.

———. *The Urbanization of America, 1860-1915.* New Brunswick, N.J.: Rutgers University Press, 1963.

McLoughlin, William G., Jr. *Revivals, Awakenings, and Reform: An Essay on Religion and Social Change in America, 1607-1977.* Chicago: University of Chicago Press, 1978.

Martin, James. *Viewdata and the Information Society.* Englewood Cliffs, N.J.: Prentice-Hall, 1982.

Martineau, Harriet. *Society in America.* 2 vols. London: Saunders & Otley, 1837.

Marx, Leo. *The Machine in the Garden: Technology and the Pastoral Eden.* New York: Oxford University Press, 1964.

Maslow, Abraham. *The Farther Reaches of Human Nature.* New York: Viking Press, 1970.

Matusow, Allan. *The Unraveling of America: A History of Liberalism in the 1960s.* New York: Harper & Row, 1984.

Merk, Frederick. *Manifest Destiny and Mission in American History: A Reinterpretation.* New York: Vintage, 1963.

Mesick, Jane Louise. *The English Traveller in America, 1785-1835.* New York: Columbia University Press, 1922.

Meyer, Donald. *The Positive Thinkers: Religion as Pop Psychology From Mary Baker Eddy to Oral Roberts.* New York: Pantheon Books, 1980.

Meyers, Marvin. *Jacksonian Persuasion: Politics and Belief.* Stanford, Calif.: Standford University Press, 1957.

Moore, Arthur K. *The Frontier Mind.* New York: McGraw-Hill, 1963.

Morgan, H. Wayne. *Drugs in America: A Social History, 1800-1980.* Syracuse, N.Y.: Syracuse University Press, 1981.

———. *Yesterday's Addicts: American Society and Drug Abuse, 1865-1920.* Norman, Okla.: University of Oklahoma Press, 1974.

Mowry, George E. *The Twenties: Fords, Flappers & Fanatics.* Englewood Cliffs, N.J.: Prentice-Hall, 1963.

Murray, Robert K. *The Red Scare: A Study in National Hysteria.* Minneapolis: University of Minnesota Press, 1955.

Nash, George. *The Conservative Intellectual Movement in America.* New York: Basic Books, 1976.

Nash, Roderick. *The Nervous Generation: American Thought, 1917-1930.* Chicago: Elephant Paperbacks, 1990.

Nelson, Daniel. *Frederick W. Taylor and the Rise of Scientific Management.* Madison, Wis.: University of Wisconsin Press, 1980.

Nevins, Allan, ed. *America Through British Eyes.* New York: Oxford University Press, 1948.

Nissenbaum, Stephen. *Sex, Diet and Debility in Jacksonian America: Sylvester Graham and Health Reform.* Westport, Conn.: Greenwood Press, 1980.

Noble, David F. *America by Design: Science, Technology, and the Rise of Corporate Capitalism.* New York: Alfred A. Knopf, 1977.

Notestein, Wallace. *The English People on the Eve of Colonization, 1603–1642.* New York: Harper, 1954.

Nugent, Walter T. K. *The Tolerant Populists: Kansas Populism and Nativism.* Chicago: University of Chicago Press, 1963.

O'Dea, Thomas F. *The Mormons.* Chicago: University of Chicago Press, 1957.

O'Neill, Gerard K. *The High Frontier: Human Colonies in Space.* New York: Morrow, 1977.

———. *2081: A Hopeful View of the Human Future.* New York: Simon & Schuster, 1981.

Parkinton, Thomas, ed. *A Casebook on the Beat.* New York: Crowell, 1961.

Paulding, James K. *The Backwoodsman, A Poem.* Philadelphia: M. Thomas, 1818.

Persons, Stow. *American Minds: A History of Ideas.* New York: Holt, Rinehart and Winston, 1958.

Pessen, Edward. *Riches, Class and Power Before the Civil War.* Lexington, Mass.: D. C. Heath, 1974.

Pickens, Donald. *Eugenics and the Progressives.* Nashville, Tenn.: Vanderbilt University Press, 1968.

Pickering, Joseph. *Inquiries of an Emigrant.* London: E. Wilson, 1839.

Pifer, Alan, and Lydia Bronte, eds. *Our Aging Society: Paradox and Promise.* New York: W. W. Norton, 1986.

Pollack, Norman. *The Populist Response to Industrial America.* Cambridge, Mass.: Harvard University Press, 1962.

Porter, Glenn. *The Rise of Big Business, 1860–1910.* New York: Thomas Crowell, 1973.

Porter, Glenn, and H. C. Livesay. *Merchants and Manufacturers: Studies in the Changing Structure of Nineteenth Century Marketing.* Baltimore: Johns Hopkins University Press, 1971.

Post, Albert. *Popular Freethought in America, 1825–1850.* New York: Columbia University Press, 1943.

Potter, David. *People of Plenty: Economic Abundance and American Character.* Chicago: University of Chicago Press, 1954.

Raschke, Carl. *The Interruption of Eternity: Modern Gnosticism and the Origins of the New Religious Consciousness.* Chicago: Nelson Hall, 1980.

Ravitch, Diane. *The Troubled Crusade: American Education, 1945–1980.* New York: Basic Books, 1983.

Riesman, David. *The Lonely Crowd.* New Haven, Conn.: Yale University Press, 1950.

Riis, Jacob A. *How the Other Half Lives.* New York: Hill and Wang, 1957.

————. *The Battle With the Slum.* New York: Macmillan, 1902.

Rodgers, Harrell R., Jr. *Poverty Amid Plenty: A Political and Economic Analysis.* Reading, Mass.: Addison-Wesley Co., 1979.

Rorabaugh, W. J. *The Alcoholic Republic: An American Tradition.* New York: Oxford University Press, 1979.

Roszak, Theodore. *The Making of a Counterculture.* Garden City, N.Y.: Doubleday, 1969.

Rothman, David J. *The Discovery of Asylum: Social Order & Disorder in the New Republic.* Boston: Little Brown, 1971.

Russett, Cynthia Eagle. *Darwin in America: The Intellectual Response, 1865–1912.* San Francisco: W. H. Freeman, 1976.

Sanford, Charles. *Quest for Paradise.* Urbana, Ill.: University of Illinois Press, 1964.

Schlesinger, Arthur M. *The Age of Jackson.* New York: New American Library, 1945.

Segal, Howard. *Technological Utopianism in American Culture.* Chicago: University of Chicago Press, 1985.

Shi, David. *In Search of the Simple Life: American Voices, Past and Present.* Salt Lake City: Peregrine Smith Books, 1986.

Singleton, Loy A. *Telecommunication in the Information Age: A Nontechnical Primer on the New Technologies.* Cambridge, Mass.: Ballinger Publishing Co., 1983.

Slater, Philip. *The Pursuit of Loneliness: American Culture at the Breaking Point.* Boston: Beacon Press, 1970.

Slotkin, Richard. *Regeneration Through Violence: The Mythology of the American Frontier.* Middletown, Conn.: Wesleyan University Press, 1973.

Smelser, Marshall. *The Democratic Republic, 1801–1815.* New York: Harper & Row, 1968.

Smith, Henry Nash. *Virgin Land: The American West As Symbol and Myth.* Cambridge, Mass.: Harvard University Press, 1950.

Somkin, Frederick. *Unquiet Eagle: Memory and Desire in the Idea of American Freedom, 1815–1860.* Ithaca, N.Y.: Cornell University Press, 1967.

Stanton, Alfred H., and Stewart E. Perry, eds. *Personality and Political Crisis: New Perspectives From Social Science and Psychiatry for the Study of War Politics.* Glencoe, Ill.: Free Press, 1951.

Stine, G. Harry. *The Hopeful Future.* New York: Macmillan, 1983.

Stoddard, Lothrop. *The Rising Tide of Color.* New York: Charles Scribner's Sons, 1920.

Stourzh, Gerald. *Alexander Hamilton and the Idea of Republican Government.* Stanford, Calif.: Stanford University Press, 1970.

Taylor, Frederick. *Principles of Scientific Management.* New York: Harper & Brothers, 1911.

Taylor, Philip. *The Distant Magnet: European Emigration to the U.S.A.* New York: Harper & Row, 1971.

Thomas, John, ed. *Looking Backward, 2000–1887.* Cambridge, Mass.: Harvard University Press, Belknap Press, 1967.

Thwaites, Reuben Gold, ed. *The Jesuit Relations and Allied Documents.* Cleveland: Burrows Bros. Co., 1896–1901.

Timberlake, James H. *Prohibition and the Progressive Movement, 1900–1920.* Cambridge, Mass.: Harvard University Press, 1963.

Tocqueville, Alexis de. *Democracy in America.* Edited by Philip Bradley. New York: Alfred A. Knopf, 1945.

Toffler, Alvin. *The Third Wave.* New York: William Morrow, 1980.

Trachtenberg, Alan. *The Incorporation of America: Culture and Society in the Gilded Age.* New York: Hill and Wang, 1982.

Trollope, Frances. *Domestic Manners of the Americans.* London: Whittaker, Treacher, 1832.

Tsiolkowski, Konstantin. *Beyond the Planet Earth.* New York: Pergamon Press, 1960.

Turner, Frederick Jackson. *The Frontier in American History.* New York: H. Holt and Co., 1920.

Tuveson, Ernest Lee. *Redeemer Nation: The Idea of America's Millennial Role.* Chicago: University of Chicago Press, 1968.

Tyler, Alice Felt. *Freedom's Ferment: Phases of American Social History From the Colonial Period to the Outbreak of the Civil War.* New York: Harper, 1962.

Tyrrell, Ian R. *Sobering Up: From Temperance to Prohibition in Antebellum America, 1800–1860.* Westport, Conn.: Greenwood Press, 1979.

Tytell, John. *Naked Angels: The Lives and Literature of the Beat Generation.* New York: McGraw-Hill, 1976.

Vatter, Harold G. *The Drive to Industrial Maturity: The U.S. Economy, 1860–1914.* Westport, Conn.: Greenwood Press, 1975.

Villoldo, Alberto, and Ken Dychtwald, eds. *Millennium: Glimpses Into the 21st Century.* Boston: Houghton Mifflin, 1981.

Wallace, Anthony F. C. *The Death and Rebirth of the Seneca.* New York: Alfred A. Knopf, 1969.

Ward, John William. *Andrew Jackson: Symbol for an Age.* New York: Oxford University Press, 1955.

Ware, Caroline Farrar. *The Early New England Cotton Manufactures.* New York: Houghton Mifflin, 1931.

Webb, Walter Prescott. *The Great Frontier.* Austin, Tex.: University of Texas Press, 1964.

White, Morton G. *Social Thought in America: The Revolt Against Formalism.* New York: Viking Press, 1949.

Whorton, James C. *Crusaders for Fitness: The History of American Health Reformers.* Princeton, N.J.: Princeton University Press, 1982.

Whyte, William. *The Organization Man.* Garden City, N.Y.: Doubleday, 1956.

Wiebe, Robert. *The Search for Order, 1877-1890.* New York: Hill and Wang, 1967.

Wood, Gordon. *The Creation of the American Republic, 1776-1787.* Chapel Hill, N.C.: University of North Carolina Press, 1969.

Wuthnow, Robert. *Experimentation in American Religion: The New Mysticisms and Their Implications for the Churches.* Berkeley, Calif.: University of California Press, 1978.

———, ed. *The Religious Dimension: New Directions in Quantitative Research.* New York: Academic Press, 1979.

Yankelovich, Daniel. *New Rules: Searching for Self-Fulfillment in a World Turned Upside Down.* New York: Random House, 1981.

Young, James. *The Washington Community.* New York: Columbia University Press, 1966.

Zopf, Paul, Jr. *America's Older Population.* Houston: Cap and Gown Press, 1986.

ARTICLES

Albus, J. S. and John M. Evans, Jr. "Robot Systems." *Scientific American* 234 (1976): 76–86B.

"American Genius and Enterprise." *Scientific American* 2 (September 1847): 397.

Bergensen, Albert, and Mark Warr. "A Crisis in Moral Order: The Effects of Watergate Upon the Confidence in Social Institutions." In *The Religious Dimension: New Directions in Quantitative Research,* edited by Robert Wuthnow, 277–295. New York: Academic Press, 1979.

Carlyle, Thomas. "Sign of the Times." *Edinburgh Review* 49 (June 1829): 439–459.

Davis, Bernard D. "The Recombinant DNA Scenarios: Andromeda Strain, Chimera, and Golem." *American Scientist* 65 (1977): 547–555.

Graham, Otis L., Jr. "The Planning Idea and American Reality: 1930s." In *The Hofstadter Aegis: A Memorial,* edited by Stanley Elkins and Eric McKitrick, 257–289. New York: Alfred A. Knopf, 1974.

Greenough, J. J. "The New York Industrial Palace." *American Polytechnic Journal* 2 (1853): 157–160.

"Improved Haymaker." *Scientific American* 5 (February 16, 1850): 184.

"Knowledge, Inventors and Inventions." *Scientific American* 5 (May 25, 1850): 38.

Lears, T. Jackson. "From Salvation to Self-Realization: Advertising and the Therapeutic Roots of the Consumer Culture, 1880–1930." In *The Culture of Consumption: Critical Essays in American History, 1880–1980,* edited by Richard Wightman Fox and T. Jackson Lears, 3–38. New York: Pantheon Books, 1983.

Leary, Timothy. "Science." In *Millennium,* edited by Alberto Villoldo and Ken Dychtwald. Boston: Houghton Mifflin, 1981.

MacDonald, Dwight. "America! America!" *Dissent* 5 (Autumn 1958): 313–323.

McGovern, James. "The American Woman's Pre World War I Freedom in Manners and Morals." *Journal of American History* 55 (September 1968): 315–333.

"Machinery and Liberty." *American Artisan and Patent Record* 1 (May 10, 1865): 2.

Marin, Peter. "The New Narcissism." *Harper's* 251 (October 1975): 45–56.

"Modern Science." *Scientific American* 3 (January 22, 1848): 67.

Morrison, Malcolm H. "Work and Retirement in an Older Society." In *Our Aging Society: Paradox and Promise,* edited by Alan Pifer and Lydia Bronte, 341–365. New York: W. W. Norton, 1986.

Morse, Samuel F.B. "Examination of the Telegraphic Apparatus and the Processes in Telegraphy." In *Reports of the United States Commissioner on the Paris Universal Exposition, 1867,* edited by William P. Blake. 6 vols. Washington, D.C.: U.S. Government Printing Office, 1867.

Murphy, Michael. "The Body." In *Millennium,* edited by Alberto Villoldo and Ken Dychtwald. Boston: Houghton Mifflin, 1981.

"The Poetry of Discovery." *Scientific American* 5 (November 24, 1849): 77.

Stanford, Charles. "The Intellectual Origins and New-Worldliness of American Industry." *Journal of Economic History* 18 (March 1958): 1–16.

Stone, Donald. "The Human Potential Movement." In *The New Religious Consciousness,* edited by Charles Y. Glock and Robert N. Bellah, 93–115. Berkeley, Calif.: University of California Press, 1976.

"The Telescope." *Scientific American* 5 (February 16, 1850): 184.

Thomas, John. "Romantic Reform in America, 1815–1865." *American Quarterly* 17 (Winter 1965): 656–681.

Turner, Frederick Jackson. "The Significance of the Frontier in American History." In *American Historical Association Annual Report for the Year 1893,* 199–227.

Walker, Timothy. "Defence of Mechanical Philosophy." *North American Review* 33 (July 1831): 122–135.

Wallace, Anthony F. C. "Revitalization Movements." *American Anthropologist* 58 (April 1956): 264–281.

"What Is the Golden Age?" *Scientific American* 5 (December 22, 1849): 109.

Index

settlement of, 9, 15, 19; in
twenty-first century, 84
Future, faith in (optimism), 22, 46,
89–90: equitable society and, ix,
8; industrialization and, 42; rein-
forcement of, 16; technology
and, 10–11; therapeutic aids for,
8–9; white, native-born Americans and, 41–42
Future, pessimism about, 89–90
Future, predicting, 27
Futurist writers, ix, 77–78

Gadsden Purchase (1853), acquisi-
tion of land through, 3
Genetic engineering, 80–82
Genetics, science of, 52
George, Henry, quoted, 56
Germany, centralized state of, 56–
57
Ginsberg, Allen, quoted, 62
Glassner, Barry, quoted, 73
Global community, 78–79, 83, 87
God, in American myth, 34–35, 38,
51, 65
Goodman, Paul, quoted, 61–62
Government, federal: centraliza-
tion of, 56, 57, 61; employment
in, 60; interest groups and, 60,
66; programs of, 70–71, 88–89;
skepticism about, 66
Graham, Otis, 58, 60–61
Graham, Sylvester, 24
Grant, Madison, quoted, 51–53
Great Depression (1930s), 4, 59–60
Great Frontier, The (1964) (Webb), 7
Greed: effects of, 2, 10, 45, 55, 57;
westward expansion and, 16–17
Greeley, Horace, quoted, 27–28
Group, power of, 61–62, 67–68
Growth, national, 2–5, 17, 38
Guards of Liberty, 30

Hakluyt, Richard, 13
Haller, Mark, quoted, 52
Harris, Louis, 66
Harris polls, 66
Health: consciousness of, 49, 73;
eating habits and, 49–50; gospel
of, 24–25, 48, 72–74
Healthy-Happy-Holy Organization
(3HO), 65
Heredity, behavior and, 52
Heroin, use of, 48
High technology, 69, 77–83
Hispanics, 17, 74, 87–88
Hoe, Richard, 35
Holding companies, 40
Hoover, J. Edgar, 53
Howe, Elias, 35
Hucksters, 27, 46, 70
Human potential therapies, 71–74
Hunter, Robert, quoted, 41

Idealism, national. See Expectations, national
Illiteracy, 68
Immigration: barriers to, 52–53, 74;
foreign, 4, 40–41, 52–53, 85, 90;
land ownership through, 14;
population increase and, 4, 85.
See also Nativism
Immorality, 22, 24–25
Individualism: advocacy of, 26, 64–
65, 71, 90–91; communications
and, 78; criticism of, 90; genetic
engineering and, 82; injustice
and, 90; loss of, 60–62, 64; Mor-
mon communalism and, 29; reform and, 28, 43. See also
Freedom, individual
Industrialists, practices of, 40
Industrialization: distribution of
wealth and, 4–5; education
and, 44; in Europe, 33–34;

People of Plenty (1954) (Potter), 7
Phrenology, 26–28
Physiological redemption, 72–74.
    See also Health, gospel of
Pifer, Alan, quoted, 87–88
Piscean Age, materialism of, 65
Political parties, 18, 86–87
Population: age of, 87–88; density,
    3, 7; distribution of resources
    and, 4–5; growth of, 3–4, 40–41,
    85, 87; urbanization and, 40–41
Pornography, 70–71
"Port Huron Statement, The"
    (1962), 64–65
Potter, David, 7–8
Poverty, 23, 41, 52, 71, 90
Practical knowledge, transmitting,
    22–23
Prevention magazine, 73
Prices, reduction in, 39–40
Printing press, rotary, invention of,
    35
Productivity, 35, 47, 80, 85
Progress and Poverty (1879)
    (George), 56
Prohibition, 47
Promise of American Life, The
    (1909) (Croly), 57–58
Prosperity, 2, 18, 50, 73
Prostitution, 20
Protein, as cause of disease, 48–49
Pushing to the Front (Marden), 45–46

Race riots of 1919, 54
Racism, 52–53, 74. *See also* Nativism
Railroads, 38, 40, 98
Ranching, 4
Ravitch, Diane, quoted, 67–68
Reagan, Ronald (president), 74–75,
    91
Reaper, mechanical, invention of
    (1834), 35

Reason, 22, 64
Reforms: control of drugs, 46–48;
    education, 21–24, 42–46, 67–70;
    health evangelism, 24–26, 48–
    51; human potential therapies,
    71–74; media influence, 69–71;
    nativism, 51–54, 28–30, 74–75;
    phrenology, 26–28; social, 80–
    81; as therapeutic aids, 8, 20–21,
    42
Relativism, 67
Religion, 29–30, 46–47, 51, 63–66, 71
Resources. *See* Material resources
Revolver, invention of (1835), 35
Riesman, David, 61
Riis, Jacob, quoted, 41
Robotics, 79–80
Rogers, Carl, 78
Russia, 36–37, 53, 68

St. Clair, Arthur, quoted, 19
Saturday Evening Post (1926), adver-
    tisement in, 50
School and Society, The (1899)
    (Dewey), quoted from, 44–45
Schoolbooks, 22, 23
Scientific American (1847, 1848,
    1849, 1850, 1860), quoted from,
    36
Scientific community, ix, 47, 66,
    82–83
Scientific management, 10, 56–57
Sectional tensions, 18
Self-help books, 45–46, 72
Senior citizens, 87, 88–89
Sewing machine, invention of
    (1846), 35
Sexual revolution of the 1960s, 70–
    71
Sexual stimulation, debilitating ef-
    fects of, 25
Shall We Slay to Eat, 49